THE

SERVANT

WAY

LEADERSHIP PRINCIPLES
FROM JOHN A. LEJEUNE

Maurice A. Buford

The views of this book are that of the author alone and do not reflect the views of the Department of Defense.

Contents

THE SERVANT WAY:

LEADERSHIP PRINCIPLES
FROM JOHN A. LEJEUNE

Conventional wisdom would suggest that one of the most prolific and capable warfighting organizations that has ever walked this planet is the United States Marine Corps. From its inception until the penning of this publication, domestic and foreign armies have traveled from the four corners of the world to study at the feet of the Corps. Civilian not-for-profits to Fortune 500 entities have collectively pondered over the secrets of the few, the proud. Though such firms marvel at the latest technology, the methodology of warfighting, and the rigor required to be a Marine, there is a more fundamental explanation to the greatness of the Marine Corps—the people who dare to join her ranks.

But it must be noted that periodically, there tends to be a personality to emerge from the crowd and demand others take note. Such an observation is typically the result of that person's commitment to excellence, that individual's pursuit of a sense of destiny, and an overall mannerism. History suggests that this personality for the Marine Corps would be the 13th Commandant—Lieutenant General John Archer Lejeune. Debatably, there has not been a more influential leader to forever shape the culture, ignite the esprit de corps, and help solidify her legacy. Though countless hallmarks are named in his honor, such as Camp Lejeune, the Lejeune Leadership Institute, and others, the literature is relatively silent when it comes to understanding the nature of this warrior's style of influencing.

In light of this gap in the literature, this publication will endeavor to answer the following questions. Was Lieutenant General John Archer Lejeune a servant-leader? What specific traits did he model during war as well as peacetime? Can this prototype help the 21st-century warrior engage the opposition, inspire the informational Marine, and motivate followership on the battlefield as well as the boardroom?

Abstracting from the original writings of Gabe (the name his friends affectionately called him) as well as other documents, Chapter One will introduce the servant-leadership construct, debunk myths, and outline Robert Greenleaf's "best test." Utilizing Greenleaf's best test to resolve the inquires of this study, Chapter Two will explore the inner workings of a servant-leader, in general, and of Lieutenant General Lejeune, in particular. Chapter Three will explore how Lejeune endeavored to grow the people who dare to hold the line as well as make the bottom line for the nation.

Chapter Four will outline the chief theories of organizational / personal "diseases" and create a conversation around Lejeune's prescription for a healthy team. Such a dialogue sets the stage to explore the servant way of making the team wiser. In other words, Chapter Five will showcase the 13th Commandant of the Marine Corps' teacher-scholar model for transforming minds. Chapter Six will explore Lieutenant General Lejeune's love for freedom and how he was able to free up others with a similar zeal. Intangible traits such as courage, critical thinking, and Lejeune's ability to create an autonomous environment will be explored in Chapter Seven. Chapter Eight examines the fundamental issue of the reactions of those being served. Stated differently, this section will drill down on the question, Were those being served by Lieutenant General Lejeune more inclined to go and serve others or defect to another brand of influencing?

Chapter Nine will demonstrate how, under Gabe's administration, the Corps was indeed no better friend, or worst enemy, globally as well as domestically. In a complimentary fashion, within the tenth chapter of this publication, attention will be turned to elements of Lejeune's blind spots as well as practical ways to mitigate them . Within the final chapter, Chapter Eleven, the sentiments of Lejeune regarding reputation will be highlighted, practical recommendations offered for the 21st-century warfighting organization are provided, and the chief research questions of this publication will be given a plausible answer.

This unorthodox journey into the historical documents of Lieutenant General Lejeune will delineate action learning questions at the end of each session. The overall intent of such a gesture is to help the reader to reflect critically, grow internally, and to encourage the servant way. As the next generation of warriors answers the call to defend this country as a United States Marine, it is imperative to abstract proven historical models to lead in the 21st century. Faddish models that advocate self-centeredness, hubris decision-making, or unethical mannerisms are short lived and ultimately undermine organizational productivity. But as history and empirical evidence demonstrates, the servant way is the prelude to greatness, legacy, and the chief mechanism to bring out the best in others. As the conversation will show, the servant way is not for the faint of heart, nor the weak in spirit, but for the disciplined. If you are ready for the challenge and are hungry for lasting transformation, consider the ensuing leadership principles from the greatest leatherneck of all time. The views of this book are that of the author alone and do not reflect the views of the Department of Defense.

CHAPTER ONE

TESTING "THE BEST TEST"

"The difference manifests itself in the care taken by the servant-first to make sure that other people's highest priority needs are being served. The best test, and difficult to administer, is..."

-Robert Greenleaf

M uch has been said about the battlefield leadership and the fighting spirit of the United States Marine Corps. But, unfortunately, the conversation goes silent when it comes down to understanding the specific influencing style of one of the most prominent Marines of all times. Virtually every Marine, or those privileged with the opportunity to serve with them, responds with the utmost respect when they hear the name of Lieutenant General John A. Lejeune mentioned. This esteem, undoubtedly, revolves around the very essence of the man, his contributions to democracy and the overall trajectory that he outlined for the Corps. But seemingly there was another intangible factor at work that energized this Marine to bring the best out of America's finest—servant-leadership.

This ability to empower followers instead of using power to dominate them (Yulk, 2002, p. 404) is perhaps one of the most misunderstood yet magnetic constructs available to foster lasting transformation. Arguably, much of the criticisms lobbed at servant-leadership are at best undergirded with baseless assertions or the result of limited research. Be that as it may, some of the chief quarrels against being a servant are worth an examination. Some of them, as outlined by Dierendonck and Patterson (2010), are as follows:

SERVANT-LEADERS ARE WEAK

As an outsider observes the servant-leadership construct at work, particularly in the context of the Marine Corps, it is a fair criticism to suggest that this model of influencing is weak. Some may consider this style soft, due to a historical management ideology that was widely employed to make workers produce. This approach to leading essentially conveyed the message that "the boss is king" and that the boss should "rule" with an iron hand. The workers were akin to "subjects" who were not entitled to express opinions, to challenge best practices, or to correct a "kingdom" that did not care for the people. In short, this model of leading is only interested in the hands of the worker (i.e., talents and manpower to achieve the bottom line) and not their hearts (i.e., the intangibles that motivate the worker). Another way to think about the traditional style of leading, which much of society tends to gravitate toward due to it being sensationalized in the media, is illustrated in Figure 1.

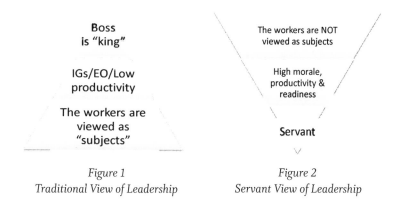

Boss
is "king"

IGs/EO/Low
productivity

The workers are
viewed as
"subjects"

The workers are NOT
viewed as subjects

High morale,
productivity &
readiness

Servant

Figure 1
Traditional View of Leadership

Figure 2
Servant View of Leadership

the boss is at the top of the proverbial triangle. Being on top implies that one is the alpha and deserves every perk that comes with being the center of gravity. For example, because these people are the principal person, they take the best space in the building even if the "subjects" recommend allowing others to work there for the sake of productivity and a gesture of morale. Because they worked hard to climb the ladder of success, these people make decisions that will make work life better and more comfortable for themselves, with total disregard for their "subject's" basic needs. This methodology of leading at first glance may appear to be good, but a closer examination of the organization may suggest something entirely different. Namely, a harder look may reveal toxic organizational symptoms such as low morale, increased sick days, an elevation of formal complaints, and a decrease in productivity.

Figure 2, in comparison, illustrates how servants respond to the approach of leading—they flip the traditional, top-down structure. Instead of viewing themselves as the king at the top of the organization and workers as subjects, the people of the entity become the chief priority. Servants create an environment that debunks the theory that the Corps is only interested in their hired hands. On the contrary, they sincerely are concerned about the matters of their heart, too (i.e., overall welfare). This cultivation of a caring organization naturally results in an elevation of morale, trust, productivity, and mission accomplishment. Moreover, instead of modeling the childhood game *king of the hill* in the workplace (the objective of this game is to make it to the top of the hill any way you can and, once there, push others down), servants choose to place themselves at the bottom (i.e., use their positional leverage) so they can help push others upward professionally and personally. This mind-set, contrary to conventional criticism, requires the strength of character, resolve, and guts to invest in the lives of America's finest.

SERVANT-LEADERSHIP IS A RELIGIOUS CONSTRUCT

The critics of this construct are quick to point out that servant leadership belongs in the religious category. The premise of this assertion revolves around the belief that echoes of this style of influencing can and should remain in the realm of the theological. Though it is true that one can find evidence of servant leaders in every major world religion, it is equally true that the servant leadership construct actually received much of its notoriety from a secular book, *The Journey to East* by Hermann Hesse. Within this short novel, a group of people travel to a specific destination. Like most groups, theirs has an array of talents, ambitions, and personalities types in the midst. One such person is simply referred to as Leo.

Leo is an unassuming and simple man. When moments of complaining emerge, he endeavors to arrange the peace. When certain tasks are required for which others have no interest, Leo quietly does them. Without fanfare, whenever there is a need, Leo makes it a point to fill it quickly. Leo's willingness and ability to serve the group empowers the team to journey as a cohesive unit.

After some time, however, Leo disappears. His abrupt vanishing has a negative impact on the team. Namely, the needs that Leo filled are gaps again. The sense of healing and optimism that he effortlessly inserted dissipates. Additionally, the journey in which they embarked seemingly becomes derailed. Out of frustration the group abandons the mission and goes their way. The story later reveals that Leo was not just an unassuming member of the team, but he was the incognito leader of the group. Moreover, the story reveals that Leo strategically planned his exodus to see if the group would embrace the ways of a servant as well as understand that within each of them resides the solution to transform the journey. It was the essence of this secular story that inspired Robert Greenleaf to advocate for the person in charge to be a servant first and then a leader.

SERVANT LEADERSHIP DOES NOT FOCUS ON THE ORGANIZATION

Another criticism of the servant leadership construct contends that such a stance means that the organization takes on a peripheral role. Stated differently, the literature seems to suggest that servants primarily focus on the overall well-being of followership. Much of their effort is dedicated to assuring that the needs of the people in the organization are supported first and that of the organization second.

The premise of this ideology, contend the critics, can potentially undermine the productivity of a firm. In the context of the Marine Corps where the chief focus is on the mission, servant leadership may appear to be a mismatch. But a closer examination of the effects of the servant way may challenge this point of view.

To illustrate, Lichtenwalner (2013) keenly observed that 50% of entities that made the top ten of *Fortune* Magazine honorees were servant-led entities. Corporations such as Southwest Airlines, Chick-fil-A, Men's Wearhouse, SAS, and others debunk the myth of servant principles not being beneficial to the bottom line. Though much of the empirical research is still in the infancy stage, the science affirms its value. For example, Baruto and Hayden (2011) found a strong relationship between this construct and perceived effectiveness, satisfaction, and extra effort. Savage-Austin and Honeycutt (2011) discovered that servant leadership had positive outcomes on improved decision making, productivity, morale, trust, and loyalty, and a reduction in employee turnover in business organizations. Moreover, Collins (2001) showed that servant leaders outperformed others in corporate America.

In light of the above, a plausible explanation may be that because servants go out of their way to build the people, the people are inclined to go out of their way to build the team. Debatably, when it comes down to warfighting, this principle gives voice to an unspoken truth in the fog of war. That is, if one were to ask Marines why they fight, the essence of their response would echo the saying—*for the Marine to my left and my right.* In other words, Marines fight because they have experienced support before the fight. Marines fight because they have confidence that the Marines around them would give the ultimate sacrifice. Marines fight for each other, and this fact empowers them to go the extra mile for the mission.

SERVANT LEADERS AREN'T ABLE TO HOLD FOLLOWERS ACCOUNTABLE

The final criticism is the belief that good order and discipline would be compromised under servant leadership. Similar to the myth of servants being weak, opponents argue that followers would essentially walk over servants, followers would not be held accountable, and followers would not be terminated for failing to adhere to organizational standards. An entire chapter will be dedicated to a Lejeune servant model of accountability. Suffice it to say that servants are very capable of exercising control discipline with followers. The point of departure, however, from traditional styles of influencing is that servants are quicker to praise in public and more inclined to reprimand in private (see Chapter Three for a more detailed argument).

THE BEST TEST

Now that a few myths have been discussed, let's turn our attention to the question, How does one determine if Lejeune was a practitioner of the servant way? Robert Greenleaf (1970), whom many credit as the champion of the theory, provides a measuring tool to help researchers make this determination. Specifically, Greenleaf indicates that

the best test is: do those served grow as persons? Do they, while being served, become healthier, wiser, freer, more autonomous, more likely themselves to become servants? And, what is the effect on the least privileged in society? Will they benefit, or at least not be further deprived?

Servant leadership test	The driving question of the best test of a servant
The growth factor	Do the served grow as persons?
The health factor	Do the served become healthier?
The wisdom factor	Do the served become wiser?
The freedom factor	Do the served become freer?
The autonomy factor	Are the served more autonomous?
The servant propensity factor	Will the served become servants?
The least factor	Will the least amongst us benefit?

TABLE 1 ROBERT GREENLEAF'S BEST TEST

As depicted in Table 1, the Greenleaf test of servant leadership examines the presence of servant leadership by way of seven probing questions or factors. The first servant indicator revolves around the question, Do the served grow as persons? The growth factor for this publication can be defined as a follower's ability to mature into a more capable, competent, and contributing citizen of an organization. Such growth may include, but is not limited to, the way servants inspire the served to take their life to the next level.

The second servant gauge deals with the health factor or trying to answer, Do the served become well? Though the concept of becoming healthier may appear to be a broad category, this element can be condensed into three distinct dimensions—physical, emotional, and spiritual health. The third servant tester pertains to the wisdom factor or understanding if the served become wiser. Wisdom can be defined as the soundness of an action or decision due to the application of experience, knowledge, and good judgment. In a complimentary manner, the fourth servant indictor asks the question, Do the served become freer? This factor explores if the served become liberated from destructive behaviors that had previously kept them living beneath their potential.

The autonomy factor is the fifth indicator of servant leadership. At this point, the served are more inclined to exercise self-government and are willing to go the extra mile for the team. Debatably, the end result of the autonomy factor is the question, Will the served become servants? This sixth measure of the existence of servant leadership is perhaps the most remarkable. It becomes significant because a life has now been transformed to transform others. As a result of this change, a paradigm shift occurs within the individual, who then becomes more concerned about the least amongst them. This final indictor of Greenleaf's Best Test is perhaps the capstone and the crowning moment of an influencer. That is, will the voiceless be heard? Can the weak be empowered, shattered lives be rebuilt, and governments of the people, by the people, be returned to the people in a better condition?

Kneecap to Kneecap Discussion

1. What is meant by the traditional style of leadership (be sure to provide examples)? Share a time in your professional career where you witnessed this in operation. Did it hurt or help the mission?

2. In your own words, define servant leadership and share how this model impacts the culture as well as the morale of the team.

3. What are the main myths affiliated with servant leadership? Please discuss in detail why you believe such perceptions were formed.

4. Who is Robert Greenleaf? Which factor of the "servant leadership test" is the most important and why?

5. As you reflect on the numerous factors of the servant leadership test, which one would you say is your strength, and which is your limitation? Be sure to explain.

CHAPTER TWO

THE AUDACITY OF A SERVANT

"The servant-leader is servant first...It begins with the natural feeling that one wants to serve, to serve first. Then conscious choice brings one to aspire to lead."

-Robert Greenleaf

I t is highly probable that the sentiments of Robert Greenleaf given in the chapter opening quote would cause the average Marine to slowly shake their head as they whispered under their breath, "Are you kidding me? Now you want us to operate in our feelings?" Well, the short answer is—a Marine already does. To explore this assertion, consider McShane and Glinow's (2013) definition of emotions: physiological, behavioral, and psychological episodes experienced toward an object, person, or event that create a state of readiness (p. 99). This state of readiness is not formulated in a vacuum. On the contrary, this mind-set can be explained logically.

Figure 3
Emotions Model

As illustrated in Figure 3, there are three closely linked variables that shape a person's being. First are the belief systems. Our beliefs are essentially our perceptions about a thing. Next are feelings. According to McShane and Glinow, feelings represent our conscious positive or negative evaluations of an object (p. 100). The final element of this model is our behavior, or the conduct that the public observes. The sum of the above may seem like an inseparable unit, but in reality, this process begins with a thought, which in turn creates an emotion, and ends with conduct. If this explanation is true, the question then becomes, What specifically are the natural feelings of a servant that leads them to want to serve, and to serve first? Patterson (2003) suggests that there are seven traits that drive the natural proclivity of a servant leader: (a) Agapao love, (b) humility, (c) altruism, (d) vision, (e) trust, (f) a serving mind-set, and (g) empowering followers.

AGAPAO LOVE

The foundational mind-set of a servant is Agapao love. In the context of leadership, Winston (2002) explains that this is a moral imperative. Namely, servants endeavor to do the right thing, at the right time, and for the right reasons. Moreover, Winston rightfully contends that this worldview, as opposed to a traditional style of leadership, views followers as hired hearts instead of hired hands. When a leader views followership merely as hired hands, then one should not be surprised when hazing, bullying, or other destructive behavior plays out in the workplace. In contrast, when American Marines, as an example, see their buddies to left and right as hired hearts (i.e., a human being worthy of self-dignity), they are motivated that much more to literally lay their life down for a friend. But let's be clear: this form of influencing is not for the weak-willed or the undisciplined. On the contrary, Agapao love is for the courageous. Patterson (2010) argues that "it is easy to rule with power and authority, based on the position one holds....Power offers an easy substitute for the hard task of love. It is much easier to control people than to love people, and yet, for the servant-leader, this is not the recipe. The servant-leader is full of love for their followers, and this changes everything. You cannot love and hurt something at the same time: if you love someone, you will care for them and care deeply; your disposition will be the evidence" (p. 73).

Perhaps this cornerstone tendency to do the right thing, at the right time, and for the right reasons is what enabled John Lejeune to inspire the Marine Corps like none other. To better illuminate Lejeune's thinking with regards to Agapao love, consider the following two reflections. First, the general believed that Agapao love created the fundamental difference for victory in combat:

> Miracles must be wrought if victories are to be won, and to work miracles men's hearts must needs be afire with self-sacrificing love for each other, for their units, for their division, and for their country. If each man knows that all the officers and men in his division are animate with the same fiery zeal as he himself feels, unquenchable courage and unquenchable determination crush out fear, and death becomes preferable to defeat or dishonor. (Lejeune, 1930, Kindle location 4134)

This fiery zeal described by Lejeune flows in two directions—horizontally and vertically. Horizontal love for their buddies to the left and right empowers them to fully commit to that intangible creed, "To never leave a Marine behind." Vertical love for the unit, division, and country allows the Marine to trust that the chain of command will always be dedicated to doing the right thing, at the right time, and for the right reasons. This form of love, contends Lejeune, has additional invaluable attributes. Namely, unquenchable courage and determination effortlessly spring forth. This overspill of Agapao is perhaps what strengthens a mother to defend her child even if the odds are against her. This excess of love is what motivates a Marine to run toward the fight and not run away. And this abundance of Agapao love is seemingly the key ingredient for organizational miracles to be wrought and for victories to be won.

An account shared by Lejeune while he visited the Division Field Hospitals is another example of this leader's understanding of the power of Agapao.

> On a bunk nearby was a Sergeant of Marines whose leg had been badly mangled by the fragments of a shell that its amputation was found to be necessary. In response to my inquiry, h⌐ told me that he had been injured by a high explosive shell just after he had crossed over the bridge over the Meuse during the last battle of the war. I asked him if he had heard before the battle that the Armistice would probably be signed within a few hours. He replied that it was a matter of common knowledge among the men. I then said, "What induced you to cross the bridge in the face of that terrible machine gun and artillery fire when you expected that the war would end in a few hours?" In answer, he said, "Just before we begun to cross the bridge our Battalion Commander, Captain Dunbeck, assembled the companies around him in the ravine where we were waiting orders, and told us, 'Men, I am going across that river, and I expect you to go with me.' The wounded man then remarked, 'What could we do but go across too? Surely we couldn't let him go by himself; we **love** [emphasis mine] him too much for that.' I have always felt that the incident I have just narrated gives one a better understanding of the meaning and the practice of leadership than do all the books that have been written, and all the speeches that have been made on the subject. (Lejeune, 1930, Kindle location 5492)

For Lejeune, the above story epitomizes the essence and the practice of leadership—love. This Sergeant of Marines could have played it safe and elected to run out the clock considering the truce was imminent. But the intangible game-changer, love, inserted itself, and the Marines gladly followed. A question that would be interesting to explore is, Would the outcome be the same if the Marines were indifferent toward Captain Dunbeck? One can only speculate. But it is a truism that beyond the trappings of rank and positional authority, Lejeune understood the critical importance of leading with Agapao. To lead without this key ingredient is analogous to serving a bride and groom their first cake without the expected sugar. It may look good from afar, but as soon as it is tasted—dismissal, disappointment, and a disrupted moment will be the order of the day.

HUMILITY

The second mentality of a servant stems from humility. This other-focused way of being should not be confused with low self-esteem or an unhealthy internalized perspective of not being good enough. On the contrary, Sandage and Wiens (2001) suggest that humility is the ability to keep one's accomplishments and talents in perspective. The antithesis of modesty is narcissism. Yulk (2010, p. 204) suggests that "narcissism is a personality syndrome that includes several traits relevant to effective leadership, such as a strong need for esteem (e.g., prestige, status, attention, admiration, adulation), a strong personalized need for power, and low emotional maturity and integrity."

Additionally, Swindoll (1981) argued that the humility of the servant is not to be equated with poor self-esteem, but rather that humility is in line with a healthy ego. In other words, humility does not mean having a low view of one's self or one's self-worth; rather, it means viewing oneself as no better or worse than others. The servant leader gains humility as a reflection of an accurate self-assessment, not self-aggrandizing or self-loathing. Therefore, a servant leader maintains a relatively low self-focus (Tangney, 2000). For Crom (1998), effective leaders are those who maintain their humility by showing respect for employees and acknowledging their contributions to the team (p. 6). On the other hand, for DiStefano (1995), humility is evident in a servant leader's acceptance of mystery and comfort with ambiguity (p. 63).

One will be hard-pressed to locate any overt gestures of humility in the primary documents of Lejeune. Due to this leader's propensity to put others above self, an analysis of other publications is brought to the reader's attention to better understand the 13th Commandant's modesty. Bates (2014), as a shining example, gauged the public's opinion on who was the greatest Marine of all time. In an unscientific poll, Bates finds that Lejeune was ranked on the bottom 2% of all famous Marines. Moreover, military history barely makes mention of Lejeune during the world war, though he led the division in some of the most savage combat (Bates, 2014). The question becomes, Why? Perhaps the ensuing quote can help to provide a plausible answer.

> Lejeune's naval career was not unlike any other Marine Officer of his time, yet he seemed to possess innate, deep-rooted, or acquired abilities to bestow, or cause to be bestowed, praise on others while reserving nothing above the simple "just doing my duty" for himself. He was neither boastful, loud, arrogant, nor unkind. Indeed, he was the exact opposite. He respected his men and paid attention to their ideas and suggestions. He gave orders and directions in a quiet, dignified manner rather than commanded. He inscribed praise

on the accomplishments of his subordinates and seniors, yet expected none and solicited none for himself. (Bates, 2014)

Lejeune never promoted or sought the spotlight for himself. This reality provides a logical explanation of why he didn't use his power to influence historical records selfishly. On the contrary, this warrior was more concerned about bestowing medals on worthy candidates and giving recognition to those under his charge that dared to serve. This virtue of the commandant, arguably, is perhaps one of his most admirable attributes.

ALTRUISM

The third attribute of a servant leader is altruism. Altruism, according to Kaplan (2000), involves helping others unselfishly. Such assistance often requires a level of personal sacrifice and does not come with a personal agenda. One can see this unselfish concern and devotion to the welfare of others on display moments before Lejeune ascended to the position of being the commandant. His predecessor, Major General George Barnett, had served in the prestigious position for four years but was relieved of duty by the Secretary of the Navy and the President of the United States. Extremely hurt by this gesture, Major General Barnett took his frustrations out on Lejeune in the presence of at least one junior officer. Moments before the official change of command, Barnett brought Lejeune to attention in front of his desk and berated him (Bates, 2014).

The record does not indicate exactly what was said out of the mouth of Major General Barnett. Nevertheless, reasonable minds can surmise that the scolding was indeed unjust, inhumane, and not kind. How did Lejeune respond? This altruistic gentleman replied by saying, "General, I will always praise your accomplishments in this office." After Lejeune became the 13th Commandant, Barnett was reduced by law to brigadier general and served his remaining time as the Commander Marine Corps Pacific Department. But immediately after the change of command, Lejeune actively sought to restore the rank of his former boss. This feat was accomplished on 5 March 1921. Any lesser person would have done the complete opposite and aggressively sought revenge. Such an account begs the question, What would you do in a comparable situation?

VISION

The fourth attribute of a servant leader is vision. Vision is essentially a picture of the future that can generate passion (Blanchard, 2000, p. 5). Additionally, influencers with vision can anticipate change and act proactively to crystalize their idea. John A. Lejeune demonstrated this attribute when he took the helm as the 13th Commandant. During this era, the nation was at a time of peace, but the Corps was restless. Such agitation, according to Bartlett (1991, p. 151), was largely because, "in July 1919, Congress cut the Marine Corps to 1,093 officers and 27,100 enlisted men. By the end of Lejeune's first year as commandant, that figure dropped to fewer than 21,000 men." It was in this context that Lejeune intuitively understood that this warfighting organization needed to see a vision for their future, something beyond the now. To this end, the 13th Commandant painted a futuristic picture so compelling that generations to this moment reap the benefits.

What were some of the fruits of Lejeune's vision? Bates (2014) suggests that Lejeune's future perspective led to the establishment of the Marine Corps Association as well as the *Marine Corps Gazette*. His insight founded the Marine Corps League, the Marine Corps birthday, and the Corps' annual celebration. Lejeune's vision mobilized the Corps to establish an institute for enlisted Marines, develop an overseas depot in World War I, and set the conditions to welcome the first female Marine to join the ranks. But perhaps his most compelling vision revolved around the war plans drafted in 1920 to conduct an amphibious war in the Pacific against Japan. It should be noted that many of the above seeds of Lejeune's vision as well as others are actively bearing fruit to this day.

TRUST

If an organization lacks trust, there can be no success. This truism was not mere words to the 13th Commandant of the Marine Corps. On the contrary, it was his core belief. Long before empirical evidence demonstrated that high-performance organizations with high interpersonal trust and highly motivated employees outperform other teams by 22% (Zak, 2017, Loc 1037), Lejeune championed the cause. One can discover trust or the positive expectations one person has toward another person in situations involving risk (McShane and Von Glinow, 2013, p. 602) outlined in the following correspondence known as *Special Trust and Confidence* written to the fleet in 1920.

> The special trust and confidence which is expressly reposed in each officer by his commission is the distinguishing privilege of the officer corps. It is the policy of the Marine Corps that this privilege is tangible and real; it is the corresponding obligation of the officer corps that it be wholly deserved.... As a concomitant, commanders will impress upon all subordinate officers the fact that the presumption of **integrity**, **good manners**, **sound judgment**, and **discretion** [emphasis mine], which is the basis for the special trust and confidence reposed in each officer, is jeopardized by the slightest

transgression on the part of any member of the officer corps. Any offense, however minor, will be dealt with promptly, and with sufficient severity to impress on the officer at fault, and on his fellow officers, the effects of the offense on the stature and reputation of the officer corps. It is an obligation to the officer corps as a whole, and transcends the bonds of personal friendship....Although this policy is expressly concerned with commissioned officers, its provisions and spirit will, where applicable, be extended to noncommissioned officers, especially staff noncommissioned officers.

An analysis of the above document will showcase the four columns that support Lejeune's notion of special trust and confidence. The first column is integrity. Covey (2006, Loc 99) explains that "integrity basically means honesty. While integrity includes honesty, it's much more. It's integratedness. It's walking your talk. It's being congruent, inside and out. It's having the courage to act in accordance with your values and beliefs." A review of the literature on Lejeune suggests this was his brightest virtue and that he expected the same from those he led. The second column associated with trust is good manners. On the surface, this value of good manners for a warfighting entity may seem like an oxymoron. Let's face it, when one thinks about destruction, chaos, and lethal engagements, the first images that surface are not those normally associated with good manners. For Lejeune, however, this is the very thing that makes a positive difference. Plainly stated, good manners are the words affiliated with a caring culture. Such words—backed up with intentional actions—convey to the team that they indeed matter and are not merely a number in the system. This fact was echoed by the Towers Watson Global Workforce Study from 29 countries. When the 32,000 followers were questioned about the most important thing a leader can do to create a high-trust organization, without fail, they pointed toward care (Vrabel, 2012).

The third column that supports trust is sound judgment. The ability to think about things clearly, calmly, and in an orderly fashion so that one can make good decisions was paramount for Lejeune. How did the 13th Commandant develop this attribute? By extension, how can others? In the book *The Reminiscences of A Marine*, Lejeune (1930, Loc 2480) provides a clue:

> The close application and the constant concentration was what I needed to systematize my mental reactions and to enable me to think connectedly, logically, clearly, and in proper sequence. Above all, the training in quick and accurate thinking produced the ability to formulate sound decisions expeditiously, and what had previously seemed difficult and laborious finally became automatic and instinctive. In this way, one acquires the military technique and, most important of all, **sound military judgment** [emphasis mine] without practicing the military art in campaigns and battles, with their accompanying hardship, suffering, danger, and death. This so-called applicatory method of instruction was one of Von Molke's greatest gifts to the military profession.

The above sentiments seem to suggest that there is a relationship between repetitions (reps) and the ability to accurately surmise the situation. In the vernacular of today's Marine Corps, a way to improve sound judgment is with relevant reps and sets. As Lejeune was exposed to applicatory instruction in the context of a military laboratory, his logic and decision-making ability crystalized. In a similar vein, other servants can elevate trust by exposing themselves to scenarios that challenge conventional thinking and force them to become a better decider.

The final column that upholds trust is discretion. The English Oxford Living Dictionary defines *discretion* as the quality of behaving or speaking in such a way as to avoid causing offence or revealing confidential information. Perhaps one of the key ways to cultivate trust is to retain those who are present, while remaining loyal to those who are absent (Covey, 2006, p. 258). This aspect of trust was best manifested in Lejeune when he became the commandant. In the article, "The Relief of General Barnett," Frank (1972) endeavored to unearth the context in which the 12th Commandant of the Marine Corps was fired. Frank does a Herculean job of answering lingering questions, and he uncovers one phrase that reveals the particular discretion of Lejeune. After the President of the United States made the decision to replace General Barnett, Lejeune arrived at headquarters to assume command. One of General Barnett's aids, Captain Clifton Cates, recounts the moment:

> General Lejeune came in. I showed him into the office, and he started to sit down. General Barnett said, "John, stand up there just a minute. We've been good friends all our lives—close friends. Why didn't you let me know what was going on?" General Lejeune replied, "George, my hands were tied." General Barnett then said, "Don't you know that if I had been in your place, I would have come to you and told you exactly what was happening?" And General Lejeune repeated, "George, my hands were tied." General Barnett then said, "Alright, I stand relieved. You're the Commandant. (Frank, 1972, p. 689)

To better understand the situation, the reader should know that Lejeune had a friendship with both the Secretary of the Navy Josephus Daniels (the one who recommended Lejeune to become the commandant) and General Barnett. If Lejeune had embraced Barnett's sentiments and tipped him off, Lejeune would have betrayed the confidence of Daniels and possibly undermined trust. As such, history suggests that Lejeune selected discretion and realized, in his own words, "my hands were tied." Every influencer who endeavors to build trust must follow carefully the path of discretion. For the sake of building trust, servant leaders must know when they have arrived at the point of tied hands.

A SERVING MIND-SET

Since the entire book is dedicated to the investigation of Lejeune's style of influencing, a brief depiction of his service will be highlighted in this section. The question becomes, How does one define serving? Wis (2002, p. 20) suggests that serving is about the utilization of "gifts and endeavors as contributing to a larger whole, much greater than themselves." Moreover, Wis adds that "Servant-leaders are not focused on displaying their gifts; rather, they use gifts to make a difference, to create positive change. In this way, they serve rather than impose; they empower rather than control."

An example of the above definition was during the Meuse-Argonne drive while Lejeune was the Commanding General of the 2nd Division. While in this position, he approached the team to engage and motivate. Though the Division was running on empty and endeavoring to recharge, they promptly came to attention. Though this is protocol in the presence of a senior officer, Lejeune quickly ordered the men to "Sit down." He went on to explain the "why" as he encouraged their fighting spirit (Asprey, 1962). "It is more important, explained Lejeune, for tired men to rest than for the Division Commander to be saluted." This illustrates that servants are more concerned about the welfare of the people and less about the stroking of their egos. As the reader will later discover, this mandate to serve rather than impose will be the central theme of this leader.

EMPOWERING FOLLOWERS

The final trait of a servant-leader that can be found in the life of Lejeune is empowerment. The ability to share authority for mission accomplishment can be found in the following quote.

> It will be necessary for officers not only to devote their close attention to the many questions affecting the comfort, health, morals, religious guidance, military training, and discipline of the men under their command but also to actively enlist the interest of their men in building up and maintaining their bodies in the finest physical condition; to encourage them to improve their professional knowledge and to make every effort by means of historical, educational, and patriotic addresses to cultivate in the hearts a deep abiding love of the Corps and Country. (Lejeune, 1930)

The 13th Commandant built a culture in which Marines would experience more self-determination, meaning, competence, and impact regarding their role in the Corps (McShane and Von Glinow, 2013). Such empowerment would be the by-product of officers devoting their close attention to the needs (i.e., questions, health, morals, religious guidance, training, and discipline) of the troops and their personal development. Not only did Lejeune set the conditions for this precept to be codified in the Corps, this Marine modeled this behavior throughout his career.

Kneecap to Kneecap Discussion

1. What is meant by "Agapao love"? How did Lejeune express this trait? In your honest opinion, is this trait in operation in today's Marine? Be sure to defend your answers with specific examples.

2. In your own words, define humility and share if you believe this trait can make a person a better warrior or not.

3. What is meant by altruistic behavior? Can this trait be developed? If so, how? If not, why?

4. Why is vision so important in the life of a leader? Discuss your thoughts on Lejeune's vision for the Corps. Also, please provide practical ways on how someone can become a better vision caster.

5. Which of the following statements best describes your belief? Be sure to defend your choice.

   Trust is given. Trust must be taken.
   Trust must be earned.

6. According to Lejeune, what are the factors that compose special trust?

7. "It is more important for tired men to rest than for the Division Commander to be saluted." Discuss in detail if you believe this ideology is in operation today. Be sure to defend your answers with examples.

8. On a scale of 1 to 5 (5 being the best), how would you grade the empowerment of followers in the Corps? Please give examples and provide ways to improve.

CHAPTER THREE

THE NINE DIMENSIONS OF LEJEUNIAN DISCIPLINE

"The Marine Corps is built on disciple and it is a rock. It is the foundation of the Corps."

-General Robert Neller,
37th Commandant of USMC

Τ he first question that a researcher must evaluate to understand if a person is a servant-leader is, Do the served grow
as persons? In order to apply this aspect of Greenleaf's "best test" to
the life of Lejeune, this chapter will not only explore whether or not
the served grew but also what the mechanism was that created such
conditions. To investigate this inquiry, several documents written
by Lejeune will be examined to provide a plausible answer. The first
explanation can be abstracted from the ensuing quote.

> Discipline, however, is the basis of military efficiency. The
> realization of the soundness of this doctrine not only caused
> the insistence on the enforcement of a strict and wholesome
> discipline with reference to both officers and men, but also
> led the Commandant to encourage the exercise of leadership
> on the part of officers of all grades by stressing the fact that the
> major factor of true military discipline consists in securing
> the **voluntary cooperation** [emphasis mine] of subordinates,
> thereby reducing the number of infractions of the laws and
> regulations to a minimum. (Lejeune, 1930, Loc 6270–6281)

THE FIRST DIMENSION OF LEJEUNIAN DISCIPLINE

LtGen Lejeune provides the reader with one of his most effective
tools for growth—discipline. Discipline, contends Lejeune, is the
basis of military efficiency. Efficiency, or organizational productivity,
hinges on the discipline factor. As outlined above, there are three
variables affiliated with the initial component of Lejeune's discipline.
The first revolves around the notion of securing the voluntary cooperation of subordinates. It can be argued that the 13th Commandant
employed four practices to achieve the intangible objective of winning the collaboration of followership. The foremost practice entailed

the constructs known as person-organization fit and person-job fit. A person-organizational mismatch occurs when the values of an individual do not align with an entity. Person-job mismatch transpires when the ability of a worker is not conducive to a position. Jim Collins' research outlined in the book *Good to Great*, would summarize such concepts by asserting that level-five leaders, which are servant-leaders, get the right people on the bus and in the right seats.

TALENT MANAGEMENT

An example of Lejeune exercising this talent management ability is with his deliberations with Earl H. "Pete" Ellis. Ellis enlisted in the Marines in 1900 and was promoted to Corporal in 1901. Corporal Ellis quickly distinguished himself and gained a reputation as being a military intellect. Such a standing coupled with congressional influence awarded him a commission in 1902 (Ballendorf and Bartlett, 1997). As a commissioned officer, Ellis continued to prove his professional mettle. This trailblazer caught the attention of Commandant William P. Biddle, and Ellis was ordered to the Naval War College in Newport, Rhode Island, where he published a series of papers, as well as became a member of the college faculty (Ballendorf and Bartlett, 1997, p. 54). Ellis continued to excel and was ordered to become the adjutant for Commandant George Barnett. It was there that John A. Lejeune, the Assistant Commandant, became acquainted with Ellis.

As the international war drums began to beat, Lejeune was ordered to France in 1917 to engage. One of Lejeune's first acts to ensure military efficiency was to get the right people on the bus and in the right seats. Who was the first person on the bus headed to the fight, and what seat did he take? When Lejeune was honored to be the first Marine to command a U.S. Army Division in combat, he took Ellis with him and made this talent the adjutant of the

Second Division. From this seat, Lieutenant Colonel Ellis earned a Navy Cross for actions rendered and contributed to the success of the war. Moreover, after Lejeune became the Commandant, he commissioned this talent to investigate what the Japanese were doing on the islands of Germany. This endeavor, undoubtedly, laid the framework for Ellis' vision of amphibious warfare to germinate as Lejeune prepared the Corps for future wars during peacetime. In sum, voluntary cooperation will naturally occur when the Pete Ellises of various organizations are placed in the right positions. In contrast, when such talent is not properly brokered, the giftedness will be utilized to disrupt the mission and increase infractions of law inadvertently.

INSPECT WHAT YOU EXPECT

The second practice employed by Lejeune to win the voluntary cooperation of the led revolves around the saying, "Inspect what you expect." The 13th Commandant states that

> In time of war, the leader must keep in touch with the current thought of his men. He must find out what their grievances are, if any, and not only endeavor to correct the faulty condition, but also to eradicate any feeling of discontent from their minds. He should **mingle freely** [emphasis mine] with his men and let them understand that he takes a personal interest in the welfare of every one of them. It is not necessary for him to isolate himself in order to retain their respect. On the contrary, he should go among them frequently so that every man in his organization may know him and feel that he knows them. This should be especially the case before battle. (Lejeune, 2016, p. 84)

From this sentiment, one can abstract several principles. Perhaps the chief of which is the admonishment of the commander to keep a finger on the pulse of the command. The objective of this pathway is to be cognizant of grievances, to proactively mitigate defective conditions, and to remove perceptions of disgruntlement.

This element of Lejeunian discipline is especially relevant in the information age. With the rise of social media to instantly broadcast disgruntlement without following protocols indigenous to the chain of command, the result could very well be a derailment. To possibly mitigate this outcome, Lejeune advises the commander to mingle freely with the team, particularly in a time of war, and especially before battle. The objective of this informal *inspecting what you expect* should not be punitive. On the contrary, the agenda of mingling is singular—to know the team and take a sincere personal interest in their overall welfare. The best way, according to Lejeune, to undermine this element of discipline is to isolate and convince oneself that their credibility will be retained without engagement. Like a religious hermit who separates themselves from the flock, so too is a commander who spends too much time in the ivory tower than in the field—they will both lose sight of the well-being of those they are called to serve.

EFFECTIVE COMMUNICATION FOR COOPERATION

The usage of effective communication is the third practice that Lejeune employed to garner the voluntary cooperation of the led. To illustrate, while mingling with the troops, the 13th Commandant suggests that

> [I]f there be no liability of the information reaching the enemy, he should take his entire organization into his confidence and inform them of the great events that are taking

place in other theatres of operations, the part being played by other units, and by their allies, if any; and give them full information on the eve of battle as to the plan of operations and the part to be played by each unit of the organization. Of course, that depends entirely whether or not the information can be kept from the enemy, if you are in reserve position, for instance. (Lejeune, 2016, p. 84)

The rapid and transparent sharing of information is a key means to ignite a team. Eisenberg, Goodall, and Tretheway (2007, p. 288) empirically demonstrated that positive in-group exchange elevates a follower's perception of organizational support as well as strengthens commitment and performance. When effective communication does not impede confidentiality, Lejeune rightly guides us to not be the leader with a secret. Ironically, the withholding of such data has a way of making its way out to the public on the proverbial grapevine with misinformation and rumors. When the chatter on the grapevine increases, research suggests that the commitment of followership can potentially decrease as well as undermine organizational discipline (Huang, 2017).

A SYMBOL OF THE FIGHTING SPIRIT

No stone should be left unturned to fill their hearts and minds with a determination to conquer, no matter what difficulties are to be overcome, and what losses they may be called on to suffer. The commander himself should be the symbol of the fighting spirit which he endeavors to foster and should show in himself a good example of patriotism, honor, and courage. (Lejeune, 2016, p. 85)

Lejeune used the power of example to mobilize the cooperation of followership. This final element, as outlined above, should be a chief priority for every commander. This is important because, during moments on the battlefield as well as the boardroom, the led will take their cues from the top. Such signals will include both what is said and what is done through actions. To this end, Lejeune argues that commanders are the symbol of the fighting spirit. A symbol can be defined as a mark or character used as conventional representation of an object, function, or process. To illustrate, when Old Glory was raised on Iwo Jima, it became a symbol of inspiration, freedom, and victory during World War II. When the troops observe their commander's words and deeds, the question becomes, What do they see? In the vernacular of today's core values, Lejeune would advise those entrusted with command to display honor, courage, and commitment (i.e., a good example of patriotism). When these attributes become more than a slogan, there is no mountain that the led would not be willing to climb for the sake of the team.

THE SECOND DIMENSION OF LEJEUNIAN DISCIPLINE

In the classic movie *300* there is a scene that best captures the second dimension of Lejeunian discipline. As Stelios balks at the Persian's request to surrender, the Persian leader replies in rage that, "A thousand nations of the Persian empire will descend upon you. Our arrows will blot out the sun!" Stelios replies, "Then we will fight in the shade!" In the next scene of the movie, the Persians make good on their threat and darken the sun with a multitude of arrows. In response, these warriors assemble side by side, raise their shields to the sky, and laughed as they remembered their leader's words. In a sense, this act captures the following ideology of the 13th Commandant.

By laying down the doctrine that the true test of the existence of a high state of discipline in a military organization is found in its cheerful and satisfactory performance of duty under all service conditions; and by reminding officers that **a happy and contented detachment** [emphasis mine] is usually a well-disciplined detachment. (Lejeune, 1930, Loc 6270–6281)

Lejeune believed an entity's ability to perform in all conditions as a happy and a contented team is a true indicator of discipline. It should be noted, however, that there is a difference between mood and the spirit of contentment (Howard and Paret, 1989). To unearth the difference, one should consider the logic of Carl Von Clausewitz. More specifically, this military mind argues that the mood of a warfighting team can fluctuate from minute to minute. The driver of such fluctuations are hinged upon questions such as: are the troops well fed or hungry, warm or cold, and so on. In contrast, "an Army with 'true military spirit' keeps its cohesion under the most murderous fire and in defeat resists fears, both real and imaginary" (Holmes, 2001, p. 600). As such, it is possible to have a happy and contented detachment that has periodic bad moods if cohesion is present. But it is not possible to pass Lejeune's true test of discipline if the mood remains depressed and there is no evidence of cohesion.

When the collective attitude remains in a negative state and cohesion is absent, history suggests that conditions become ripe for mutiny, defeat, or some other tragic mishap. How then should a commander implement this dimension of Lejeunian discipline and proactively mitigate such adverse conditions? Again, we turn to Clausewitz to offer an explanation.

The first is a series of victorious wars; the second, frequent exertions of the army to the utmost limits of its strength. Nothing else will show a soldier the full extent of his capacities. The more a general is accustomed to place heavy demands on his soldiers, the more he can depend on their response. A soldier is just as proud of the hardships he has overcome as the dangers he has faced. In short, the seed will grow only in the soil of constant activity and exertion, warmed by the sun of victory. Once it has grown into a strong tree, it will survive the wildest storms of misfortune and defeat, and even the indolent inertia of peace, at least for a while. Thus, this spirit can be created only in war and by great generals, though admittedly it may endure, for several generations at least, even under generals of average ability and through long periods of peace. (Howard and Paret, 1989, p. 276)

An analysis of Clausewitz's sentiments suggest that the waging of victorious wars and the practice of frequent exertions are the keys to cohesion. The art of winning battles and constantly pushing beyond limits are the key elements to create a happy and contented detachment. If a commander lacks, however, the personnel who have experienced battle, then "it is especially advisable, whenever it can be done, for the commander to assemble his troops by battalions and address them, telling them of the great traditions and history of their organization and appealing to their patriotism and their esprit de corps (Lejeune, 2016, p. 85). This art of storytelling coupled with the prudent, yet intentional push of limitations, will yield the form of discipline that propels the troops to jovially fight in the shade.

THE THIRD DIMENSION OF LEJEUNIAN DISCIPLINE

The third dimension of Lejeunian discipline centers on grooming standards. While operating on the conventional wisdom of the time, the 13th Commandant believed that well-dressed soldiers are usually well-behaved (Lejeune, 1930, Loc 6281). That is, if a servant of the state took the time to be well groomed and dressed, their propensity to misbehave drastically decreases. As fate would have it, this principle has recently been empirically validated. To illustrate, Adam and Galinsky (2012) demonstrated in their experiment that when participants wore attire that projected authority or presence, it positively impacted their conduct. Such an effect was termed *enclothed cognition*. Enclothed cognition describes the systematic influence that clothes have on the wearer's psychological processes. As such, Lejeune restored "the blue uniform, to the successful endeavor to include American manufacturers to produce a khaki cloth of high grade both as texture and dye, and to improvements in the design and the cut of all articles of uniform" (Lejeune, 1930, Loc 6277). This decision, undoubtedly, elevated morale and softly mitigated self-destructive behaviors of a peacetime Corps.

THE FOURTH DIMENSION OF LEJEUNIAN DISCIPLINE

The fourth dimension of Lejeunian discipline is close order drill. While at the Naval Academy, Lejeune "acquired the rudiments of military training, as we were instructed daily in close order drill up to and including the School of the Battalion, and in the ceremonies of Dress Parade and Guard Mounting, following with almost religious punctilio the rules and regulations prescribed in Upton's Military tactics....My experience at the University was not only of great benefit to me from the standpoint of mental training and education, but was of even greater advantage because of the physical training, the discipline, and the habits of military obedience and military command which were inculcated there" (Lejeune, 1930, Loc 325). The current USMC Corporal's Course lesson best explains the intent of this construct by stating that

> The purpose of close order drill is to enable a commander to 1) move the unit from one place to another in a standard, orderly manner, while maintaining the best appearance possible. 2) Provide simple formations from which comb't formations may be readily assumed. 3) Teach discipline by instilling habits of precision and automatic response to orders. 4) Increase the confidence of his junior officers and of his noncommissioned officers through the exercise of command, by giving the proper commands and the control of drilling troops. 5) Give Marines an opportunity to handle individual weapons. (Corporals Program, 1999)

From the literature on leadership's perspective, it takes a sequence (sets) of repetitions (reps) to become an expert. More specifically, Gladwell (2008) argues that one must invest 10,000 hours to become a professional in a craft. This logic can also be applied to the discipline factor. For Lejeune the countless hours that was placed in close order drill yielded not only an orderly Marine, but an influencer whose impact will be felt for generations to come.

THE FIFTH DIMENSION OF LEJEUNIAN DISCIPLINE

While reflecting on the success at the battle of Waterloo, LtGen Lejeune invoked the ideology of a famous strategist to unearth the fifth dimension of discipline. More specifically, the 13th Commandant stated that

Lord Wellington is supposed to have said that the battle of Waterloo was won on the cricket fields of England. A paraphrase of this saying to fit the needs of the Marine Corps could readily be provided, but it is unnecessary to do so, as I believe it to be almost universally accepted as sound policy that the cultivation of athletics in a military organization is extremely beneficial to the personnel from the standpoint both of improved physique and improved morale. For these reasons, a comprehensive athletic policy for the Marine Corps was adopted and put into effect, and athletic activity, especially in connection with football and baseball, everywhere prevailed. (Lejeune, 1930, Loc 6287)

It was as if Lejeune understood that cohesion could be built in the "laboratory" of athletic endeavor. For it is on the fields that a commander can help set the conditions for a unit to navigate the stages of group formation as described by Tuckman (1977). The stage includes forming (which is characteristic of uncertainty and confusion), storming (conflict is constant), norming (collaboration becomes the norm), performing (fully functioning team), and adjourning (termination of the team). If a unit is required to suddenly go from phase 0 to phase 3, as an example, the battlefield is not the place to graduate to the performing stage where cohesion would be lacking. As pointed out by Lejeune, solidity can possibly be expedited if a commander incorporates sports. This modest emphasis, as Lord Wellington knew, could be the difference between victory and defeat.

Kelinske, Mayer, and Chen's (2001) research adds to the conversation by amplifying the benefits of sports from a scientific perceptive. To illustrate, Kelinske et al. sampled 117 participants to understand their perception of the benefits of engaging in athletics. The sample indicated that participation in sports refines moral reasoning, socialization, competition, health, and fitness, and improves leadership skills. If in fact sports can cultivate cohesion and bring out such attributes, then it is a logical inference to suggest that commanders should pay more attention to the fifth dimension of Lejeunian discipline.

THE SIXTH DIMENSION OF LEJEUNIAN DISCIPLINE

The sixth dimension of the Lejeunian discipline revolves around good will. Lejeune indicates that

While the Marine Corps Expeditionary Force, when landed in a foreign country, is primarily intended to protect the lives and property of American citizens residing there during periods of disorder; it is also intended to benefit and not to oppress the inhabitants of the country where it is serving. This altruistic conception of the duties of Marines was constantly impressed on the officers and men stationed abroad, with the result that the good will of the law-abiding people with whom they were associated was gained and peace and good order were restored and maintained. (Lejeune, 1930, Loc 6301)

This notion of foreign nations benefiting from the altruism of Marines is paramount. Good will efforts, such as building schools, feeding the hungry, and providing medical care for the sick, can indeed help to win hearts and minds. In contrast, when service members engage in selfish and intentionally destructive behaviors, the reputation of the nation can literally hang in the balance.

On the surface, it may seem counterproductive for warfighters to also see themselves as ambassadors of philanthropy (i.e., employing acts of good will that doesn't undermine the mission), but that is exactly Lejeune's point. Marines can be both—and not just either/or. Moreover, not only can the employment of good will build capital with foreign nations, it can also contribute to the second dimension of Lejeunian discipline—a happy and contented detachment. Dunn, Aknin, and Norton's (2002) research illuminates the point. While studying the behaviors of 632 participants, Dunn et al. discovered that when the sample gave to others, they were happier. Thus, validating the adage—it is more blessed to give than to receive. When the troops exercise good will, it can contribute to their overall contentment. As alluded to before, when Marines are content, their fighting spirit cannot be conquered nor will their nation be ashamed of their actions.

THE SEVENTH DIMENSION OF LEJEUNIAN DISCIPLINE

The seventh dimension of Lejeunian discipline focuses on commendation. Commendation, or the ability to sincerely recognize a follower for their efforts, can be an instrumental tool of motivation. Lejeune believed that

Following the battle, it is well, too, to issue an order of recounting the exploits of the troops and telling them of the effects of their efforts. At this time the men are exhausted in mind and body, even though they may have been victorious, they are depressed in spirit on account of the many losses they have suffered…every effort should be made to cheer and raise their spirits. Praise and commendation should be given freely; decorations should be promptly awarded and delivered immediately after withdrawal from the front lines. Addresses to organizations which have distinguished themselves should be made. Replacements should be furnished promptly, if practicable, and the thoughts of the men immediately turned to building up their shattered organizations and preparing again to strike the enemy. (Lejeune, 2016, p. 85)

An analysis of the above quote unearths seven inspiring principles that can help to grow an organization. The first entails the writing of orders that essentially speaks to the "why" as well as the "so what" of an engagement. When the proverbial dots are not clearly connected in the minds of a warrior, the conditions for cognitive dissonance can be inadvertently created. When cognitive dissonance (the state of having conflicting thoughts, beliefs, or attitudes, especially as relating to behavioral decisions and attitude change) persists, a mental fog can ensue, which leads to self-destructive behaviors. As such, Lejeune admonishes influencers to issue an order that essentially captures the effects and efforts of the team. In other words, after a campaign is waged, a commander should write a letter of commendation to a battalion or company that clearly explains how their specific struggles, big or small, contributed to the fight. Why is this important? Research on the best practices of Western warfighting indicate that a leading variable of a successful campaign is a unified belief in the cause (Holmes, 2001, p. 600). As such, when an influencer clearly articulates the "so what," it can contribute to followers' ability to focus.

Another inference that one can abstract from the above quote is that a caring and commending culture can help to address the physical, emotional, and mental fatigue that's affiliated with battle. The crux of this second component of the seventh dimension of Lejeunian discipline endeavors to effectively cheer and raise the spirits of the team. When this measure is employed, it can proactively mitigate the effects of PTSD. This assertion is not made in a vacuum but rather on the foundation of emerging research. More specifically, Castro et al.'s (2006) research with 1,146 soldiers found that when warriors were exposed to Battlemind training (the Army's version of holistic caring), soldiers better navigated the transitions from the combat zone to home.

The third principle that is highlighted from this section spotlights the need and speed factor. That is, Lejeune advocates that if there is a legitimate need to affirm a warrior for actions rendered and if it is in the power of a leader to do so, that servant should act. Often in the context of today's organizations, conventional wisdom suggests that it is best to wait for a special occasion or to perhaps wait for the next quarterly event to give honor to whom honor is due. Though this practice is not necessarily wrong, it does, however, lose some of its power. The impact diminishes as more time separates the actor from the deed. This space, if left to its own devices, can, unfortunately, be filled with negative self-talk and organization griping, which can subsequently undermine discipline. To mitigate such negativity, Lejeune contends that the speed of commendation should be set to promptly and immediately. While reflecting on the best practices of the American Allies, Lejeune (2016, p. 85) suggests that, "The French, I think, understood the psychology of their people from the way they lined up their troops and decorated them immediately after they came out of the fight." Scientifically speaking, Zak's (2017) research revealed that entities who regularly celebrate their people enjoy lower turnover rates, higher productivity, and increased levels of organizational trust. Hence, the psychology of rewards can be summarized by the saying, "Whatever you appreciate, will appreciate in the organization."

Practically speaking, the question becomes, Are there particularly effective ways to appreciate organizational citizens for their efforts? Chapman and White (2011) would suggest that there are five languages that a leader can employ to motive the led. The first language is words of affirmation. An example of this language in the context of the military is offering Bravo Zulu (BZ) or words that convey, "Well done." In other words, a leader finds the led doing something positive and sincerely expresses gratitude for extraordinary performance. The second language is quality time. That is, an influencer carves time out of their schedule and sets up a professional meeting with a follower for purposes of mentoring. The third language is acts of service. The recipient of such encouragement is gratified by witnessing others simply "jumping in" and helping to "get things done." Fourth is the offering of gifts. In the context of the military, the operative word would be *legal gifts*. An example of this may be the giving of a day off or liberty. The final language that a leader can invoke to encourage the team is physical touch. Again, physical touch in the context of government may include a firm handshake, an acceptable pat on the back, or in the face of an unfortunate mishap, an appropriate hug. The key, contends Chapman and White, is to understand the preferred language of the led and speak it. It should be noted that it costs a servant nothing to "speak" one of these languages, but it will be very costly to the team if the message is withheld.

The fourth principle that can be garnered from this section is the usage of speeches. To recap, Lejeune argues that, "addresses to organizations which have distinguished themselves should be made." In a sense, Lejeune is arguing that leaders should assemble the teams that have made a positive impact on the mission and convey publicly their sincere gratitude on behalf of a grateful nation. This form of public team ovation is the very thing that research suggests followers desire from leaders. Namely, Hickman (1998) found that followers want their leaders to be less of a hero and more of a hero maker. One aggressive step to become more of a hero maker is to address those organizations that have distinguished themselves.

The fifth ideology of Lejeune revolves around the furnishing of replacements. The inference of this principle suggests that in battle, Marines will die. When this happens, a commander is compelled to provide replacements for two reasons—cohesion and mission accomplishment. A commander has the responsibility of being the resource allocator. Within this role, the leader has the responsibility to decide the who, what, when, why, and where of manpower. To this end, and in the face of fatalities, the priority should be on the replacement factor. Though choices may be limited, this gesture when directed to a team fresh from the fight can contribute to the raising of morale. In a similar vein, such a decision point can help to maintain the momentum of mission accomplishment.

Without question, when a brother or sister in arms passes away, it can have a negative impact on the command. At such times, Lejeune admonishes leaders to turn their attention to the building up of shattered organizations. This sixth principle of inserting resilience (see Chapters Four and Fourteen for a more detailed analysis) acknowledges a fundamental belief—Never leave a Marine behind. This phrase, in the context of this section, suggests that if a brother/sister falls, that member will be honored. Moreover, in their memory the team will rebuild and emerge as a more lethal warfighting organization.

The final principle that one can abstract from this section speaks to the very mission of the Corps. Namely, Lejeune suggest that leaders should prepare again to strike the enemy. This can be done, according to the 13th Commandant, by staying razor focused on the ultimate mission of the Corps. Such a focus in and of itself can serve as a synergistic catalyst of transformation. After all, who would not be motivated to be a part of "America's expeditionary force in readiness since 1775, the Marines are forward deployed to win our nation's battles swiftly and aggressively in times of crisis. They fight on land, sea and air, as well as provide forces and detachments to naval ships and ground operations." To this end, the preparation to fight is a commendation tool in and of itself if done correctly.

Category of Offense	The Speed
Cowards & Skulkers—Cat 1	Promptly
Commission—Cat 2	Prudently
Careless Omission—Cat 3	Patiently

TABLE 2 LEJEUNE'S CATEGORIES OF PUNISHMENT

THE EIGHTH DIMENSION OF LEJEUNIAN DISCIPLINE

The eighth dimension of Lejeunian discipline emphasizes account-ability. The breadth of Lejeune's writings and deliberations seems to suggest that there are three instances in which a servant should hold a follower accountable. The following quote unearths the first category:

Skulkers and cowards should be promptly and publicly pun-ished so that all may see the great gulf which separates them from the gallant men who have served faithfully and cou-rageously. One is just as important as the other. The way it appealed to me overseas is that there were three classes of men. The first class, [were] the gallant, courageous fellows who did not require any urging or any leadership practically, but who from a sense of duty, loyalty, and patriotism would stay up in the front lines and fight until all hell froze over. And the third class, [were] the skulkers, the white-livered fellows whom you could not expect anything of at all. Then there was a great middle class who could be swayed either way, and that was the class you had to deal with. If the ser-vices of the men who fought bravely were not promptly and properly recognized on the one hand, and if the skulkers and cowards were not punished on the other, the sentiment might grow that it was just as well to skulk. You got nothing for not doing your duty. The two go hand in hand, and punishments should be prompt and merciless to a real coward. (Lejeune, 2016, p. 85)

The spirit of this quote seems to suggest that Lejeune viewed cowards and skulkers as cancers to organizational health. When a person allows the natural fear that is affiliated with war to overpower their training, this can potentially unravel the fiber of command. When left unchecked, this refusal to confront the hardships of combat and the possibility of injury and death (Holmes, 2001) can lead to dereliction of duty.

If a commander exercises laissez-faire leadership and does nothing, the message conveyed to the gallant will be problematic. Hence, Lejeune advises for a prompt and public punishment to be delivered to cultivate organizational health. It should be noted that this prompt and public punishment is not a new phenomenon. On the contrary, the Roman army had a standard that required a unit found of cowardice to be paraded in front of the legion and every tenth man subjected to a *fustuarium* or a form of harsh military punishment (Holmes, 2001). Perhaps this first category of Lejeunian discipline was a soft attempt to bring to pass the sentiments of Frederick the Great in the hearts of the command. Frederick the Great believed that the common soldier must fear his officer more than the enemy. Whether or not that was Lejeune's intent is unknown, but what is clear is the principle. It would serve commanders well in today's context to find the equivalent and appropriate public and prompt lever to mitigate cowardly ways in today's fighting units.

An examination of the body of Lejeune's work seems to suggest that the second category of punishment revolves around acts of commission. Acts of commission include willful deeds of a member that are understood to be wrong before they engage. Like most acts of commission, there is often a cloud of ambiguity and negative press affiliated with the alleged incident, as was the case of the unproven war crimes in Haiti on Lejeune's watch. Upon assuming the mantle of leadership for the Corps, a New York newspaper, *The Nation*, accused Marines in Haiti of abuse and improper conduct. Instead of delegating the task to others or relying on hearsay, Lejeune sought and received permission from the Secretary of the Navy to personally travel to investigate the matter. Though it was reported that the commandant would travel to South Carolina to conduct the business of the nation, Lejeune boarded a ship and sailed to Haiti and Santo Domingo without fanfare (Lejeune, 1930, Kindle Loc 6301). During his personal investigation, he learned that there were indeed infractions, which resulted in court-martial. However, those cases didn't align with the report found in *The Nation*. As such, the prudence of Lejeune was able to mitigate a public image crisis.

The third category of Lejeunian punishment revolved around careless acts of omission or general misconduct. It is interesting to note that research suggests that 93% of all workforce disciplinary issues occur at this juncture (Moss, 2013). It is at this place that an influencer is encouraged to exercise patience and adhere to the following counsel.

> Discipline, in its true sense, should never be neglected. The men should be made to realize its great importance, but in enforcing it, officers should never be harsh or arrogant in their dealings with their men, but always kind, humane, and just. (Lejeune, 2016, p. 85)

In no wise does Lejeune admonish the withholding of discipline. On the contrary, the 13th Commandant makes a case that it should be done in a servant way. More specifically, when employing discipline on a follower, Lejeune advocates that it should not be done from the premise of harshness or arrogance. To be cruel implies that the giver of punishment is at a heightened state of irritation. Typically, when a person is operating at this level, they engage to bring themselves to a place of relief. In other words, instead of employing discipline to correct a deficiency in a follower, they flex to make themselves feel better.

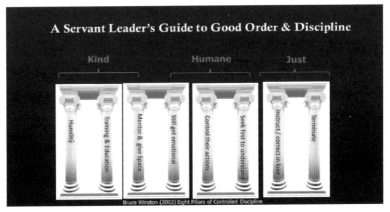

Figure 4 The Eight Pillars of Controlled Discipline based on Winston's (2002) Research

KIND

In a similar way as being cruel will thwart effective leadership, arrogance or being full of oneself will undermine a leader's ability to correct deficiencies. To be arrogant implies that one has never made a mistake. Arrogant people are not teachable for they feel they are the smartest people in the room, and their perspective is the only way to view things. These two positions can make matters worse and can potentially backfire by engendering lawsuits, violence, and organizational stagnation. As such, Lejeune contends that leaders should deliver discipline with a kind, humane, and just spirit. If this is true, the question arises, Does the leadership literature operationalize such traits?

A construct known as controlled discipline aligns with the sentiments of Lejeune. Winston (2002) suggests that controlled discipline points toward an influencer's ability to effectively govern one's personal behavior. More specifically, controlled discipline or self-control is undergirded by eight pillars as depicted in Figure 4. The first three pillars fit well with Lejeune's notion of being kind or demonstrating sincere care to another. When a follower stands before a servant-leader to receive correction, the first characteristic displayed is humility. In contrast to engaging with an arrogant disposition, a servant realizes that but by the grace of God, there goes I. This temperament helps one to remain teachable and reachable. These two qualities—teachable and reachable—can help with the collection of facts before a decision is made. Moreover, humility helps a leader to understand that the agenda of discipline is a regular function of supervisors to help employees learn what to do and how to think (Buford, Gomez, Patterson, and Winston, 2014) and not a means to make the leader feel better.

The second pillar is training and education. Namely, most discipline problems emerge because the follower does not adequately understand what is expected. To this end, influencers go out of their way to mitigate the knowledge gap by investing in the training and education of the led. It may be true that a follower who holds a position has never adequately been trained to succeed in the role.

To mitigate the knowledge gap, leaders should constantly grow the force with competency specific learning. In a complimentary fashion, Winston's (2002) third pillar advocates for mentoring and creating space as well as opportunities for growth. This form of investing helps followers understand that the organization is vested in their success and can renew the motivation of the person who made a careless act of omission.

HUMANE

LtGen Lejeune believed that being humane was a central variable to correcting others. *Humane* can be defined as having or showing compassion or benevolence. Considering this definition, Winston's (2002) argument makes sense. Namely, it is a natural and human passion to become emotional in the discipline moment. In fact, research suggests that disciplining a follower can impact one's health. Mittleman's study (as cited in the Associated Press, 1998) revealed that a sizable percentage of heart attacks occurred during the moment of holding others accountable. This reality implies that leaders should take heed of their health in such a moment, confirming the validity of Winston's third pillar that servants still get emotional. This passion in and of itself is not the problem. It is the human predicament.

However, how well one regulates such passion will determine if their actions will be cruel or humane. Buford's (2012) research discovered that leaders employed several best practices to actualize Winston's (2002) fifth pillar of controlling their actions. The first practice revolved around the participant's spirituality. Namely, leaders would petition their higher power for wisdom and peace as they process the situation. The second practice dealt with taking an intentional pause before proceeding to a decision point. This endeavor helps the participants to recalibrate to a place of being level-headed. The third habit included coaches, mentors, and role-models. That is, the leaders of Buford's study would reach out to personalities that impacted their lives in a positive way and vent to them. This process seemingly helped them to clear their thinking as well as to control their actions. The final best practice involved the usage of self-talk. More specifically, the participants of the study would remind themselves of leadership principles or other inspiration points to help them recenter.

Upon navigating through the emotions of discipline and arriving at a place of regulation, a leader is then empowered to be more of a listener. It is at Winston's (2002) sixth pillar that servants learn to ask the right probing questions to better comprehend the why of a follower's behavior. For example, if a Marine is constantly late for formation, it may help to explore the family or financial dynamics. Such a line of questioning may surprisingly reveal that the Marine is not a slacker but arrives late because his personal vehicle is broken. As a result, he decided to use the public transportation (that is not dependable) and elected to keep that information from the chain of command out of fear.

JUST

Conventional wisdom recalls the notion of justice when thoughts of discipline emerge. For Lejeune, being just was indeed a critical component of the process, and being just followed being kind and humane. The process of behaving according to what is morally right and fair is perhaps the crux of the punishment moment. In Winston's (2002) model, there are two variables affiliated with being just. Pillar seven calls for a leader to instruct and correct in love. In other words, after the previous columns have been exhausted, clear directives should be issued to mitigate the deficiency. It should be noted that such a process must be proportional to the offense and done in a spirit of love and, again, not with cruelty. If such a process does not correct the shortcoming of the follower, and assuming that a leader has navigated Winston's previous pillars successfully, the last course of action is termination of service.

THE NINTH DIMENSION OF LEJEUNIAN DISCIPLINE
Regardless of the terms in which a Marine departs the Corps, Lejeune believed there is a psychological contract at play. Namely, the obligation of the Corps is to foster the following principle.

> The recognition of this responsibility on the part of officers is vital to the well-being of the Marine Corps. It is especially so for the reason that so large a proportion of the men enlisting are under 21 years of age. These men are in the formative period of their lives and officers owe it to them, to their parents, and to the Nation, that when discharged from the service they should be far better men physically, mentally, and morally than they were when they enlisted. (Lejeune, 1920)

This statement abstracted from his famous *Special Trust and Confidence* order, points toward the value of returning America's young adults back to society as better citizens in three distinct ways. First, the Corps and the nation have an obligation to care for veterans that may have experienced loss of life, limbs, or invisible wounds such as PTSD. Second, the custodians of warfighting should see to it that returning servicemen receive a formal education or a trade to help them successfully integrate back into society. Finally, their experiences as a warfighter should make them more of a moral leader and equipped to make a positive impact in their chosen professions once they remove the uniform. When this unwritten contract is violated, it can undermine the credibility of the Corps and impact future standard operating procedures.

CONCLUSION

Let's now return the reader's attention back to the first part of Greenleaf's "best test" and provide a feasible answer to the question, Did the Corps grow under the 13th Commandant and what mechanism did he utilize to achieve this feat? As outlined above, nine dimensions of discipline were invoked to not only create a permanent seat in the mental models of the country, but such discipline was also chiseled in the hearts of those who dared to serve. As discussed in Chapter 1, it was because of Gabe's servant way that publications were created, educational opportunities established, and today's Corps benefits from his vision like no other Marine. To this end, one would have to accept the logical argument that John A. Lejeune indeed grew the Corps mainly with good order and discipline. The question now becomes for the reader, How well are the people under your charge growing, and what mechanism are you utilizing?

Kneecap to Kneecap Discussion

I was told once; the Marine Corps is built on disciple and it is a rock. It is the foundation of the Corps. And every time you walk by something you know is wrong, it is the equivalent of taking a hammer and hitting the rock and putting a chip in it. And if enough people walk by, pretty soon the rock is going to crack...So we maybe at that point. *General Robert Neller at Senate Hearing 17 March 2017.*

    1.   Think about General Neller's above comments to the Senate. On scale of 1 to 5 (five being the highest), how would you

rate the strength of the discipline rock in your organization? Be sure to provide examples with your score.

2. Robert Greenleaf's first aspect of his "best test" question revolves around how well those under the leadership are growing. While considering this, how would you rate yourself? What do you need to do to improve?

3. In your own words, define *discipline* and share a time when you received this in a positive and negative manner.

4. Which one of the nine dimensions of Lejeunian discipline resonates the most with you and why?

5. Which dimension of Lejeunian discipline are you the weakest in, and the strongest? Please explain with someone else.

REVIEWING
STAND
COMMANDER
IN CHIEF

 CHAPTER FOUR

THE G.R.I.T. OF
A SERVANT

*"Esprit de corps and morale are kindred subjects; in fact,
some writers consider them as synonymous. This, however,
is not the case, as esprit de corps is only one of the factors
which goes to constitute morale. Morale is three-fold—
physical, mental or professional, and spiritual."*

-John A. Lejeune

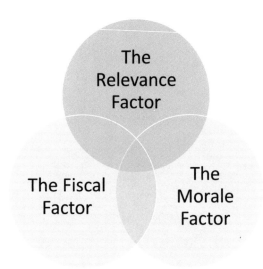

Figure 5 The 1920–1929 Marine Corps
Organizational Health Factors

T he second question that a researcher must gauge to determine whether or not a person is a servant-leader is, Do the served become healthier? To wrestle with this question, the reader should understand the realities and historical context in which Lejeune entered the office of the commandant. On June 20, 1920, Lejeune was promoted to the rank of Major General and took the helm as the 13th Marine privileged as well as responsible for the Corps. This period marked an era of peace in the American experience at the twilight of World War I. As is the historical case during the aftermath of war, calls for normalcy became the order of the day. Unfortunately, such calls also invoked turbulent winds of change at the homefront.

A cursory examination of military history will reveal that there were three overarching threats to the organizational health of the Corps during Lejeune's tenure. As depicted in Figure 5, the first hazard related to the whispers of relevance. More specifically, from the initial ideology of George Washington up until the tenure of Lejeune, questions were constantly asked either literally or through the inactions of administrators, Why do we need a Marine Corps? Lejeune was very acquainted with this disposition and particularly experienced it while in command of the 2nd Division. During this time, for example, the sentiment of significance was packaged in an order issued by General John J. Pershing. This Army Commanding General provided the guidance during the engagement of World War I that by no means would specific units receive media coverage (Bartlett, 1991, p. 69). This order was curious since a Marine for the first time had the honor to lead an Army Division in combat. This guidance revealed a sentiment that would not fully be resolved until well after the tenure of Lejeune.

The second factor that challenged the organizational health of the Corps under Lejeune were fiscal factors. "In July 1919, Congress cut the Marine Corps to 1,093 officers and 27,100 enlisted men. By the end of Lejeune's first year as commandant, that figure dropped to fewer than 21,000 men" (Bartlett, 1991, p. 153). Though all the services experienced proportional cuts, this rollback may have reignited the whispers of relevance as well as contributed to the third threat of organizational health—the morale factor. The smoking gun of low morale prior to Lejeune becoming the commandant was the presence of cancerous silos. Lencioni argues that

> Silos are nothing more than the barriers that exist between departments within an organization, causing people who are supposed to be on the same team to work against one another. And whether we call this phenomenon departmental politics, divisional rivalry, or turf warfare, it is one of the most frustrating aspects of life in any sizable organization....In most situations, silos rise up not because of what executives are

doing purposefully but rather because of what they are failing to do. (2006, p. 92)

What were the silos of Lejeune's era? According to Norton (2008), there were three distinct factions in operation—the graduates of the Naval Academy, the Bushwhackers, and the WWI Veterans. The graduates of the Academy were perceived to be intellectuals that lacked battlefield experience. The Bushwhackers were those Marines who had primarily engaged in small wars (i.e., Banana, colonial occupations, etc.), and the veterans of WWI were depicted as the face of the military during that era. The sum of the above threats to organizational health with an emphasis on silos began to negatively impact the Corps. Namely, the perfect storm of internal as well as external issues made it difficult to revitalize organizational efficiency, retain talented Marines, and recruit future warfighters. Considering such wicked problems, Lejeune

> Adopted as the guiding principle of [his] administration the rule that the good of the Corps, combined with the just treatment of all officers and men, was paramount and, therefore, took precedence over all other considerations. The practice of this principle precluded the exercise of favoritism and brought about among the officers and men a feeling of confidence in the administration of Marine Corps affairs. The spirit of unity and confidence which prevailed made it possible to put into effect many beneficial policies in the direction of increased military efficiency. (Lejeune, 1930, Loc 6258)

The question now becomes, How specifically did Lejeune operationalize the above guiding principle and thereby improve the health of the Corps? The following acronym captures the 13th Commandant's best practices to increase military efficiency:

Garbage can—the broken window theory

Reach 10,000 reps and sets

Infuse spiritual fitness

Transparently go the extra mile

GARBAGE CAN: THE BROKEN WINDOW THEORY

A theory birthed by James Q. Wilson and George L. Kelling endeavored to capture the psychology of deviant behavior. More specifically, these theorists asserted that if a few windows on a building were not repaired, it would quickly set the conditions for increased negative patterns. To mitigate this mind-set, influencers, asserts the theorists, should expeditiously course-correct minor issues before they blossom into an uncontrolled ordeal. Though there were no literal broken windows on the planes of the Corps, there were, however, psychological cracked windows floating around in the minds of Marines that threatened organizational health. Lejeune understood this reality and quickly implemented directives for the purposes of producing some small wins.

According to Kotter (2012), small wins are essential to the art of leading change. Kotter's research suggest that short-term wins have three traits. First, they are visible. It is at this place that an organization can judge for themselves if a leader is the real deal or just hype. Second, the small win is unambiguous. That is, the accomplishment is not a metaphorical tie or a fluke. Third, the small win is clearly related to the change effort. Moreover, Kotter argues that short-term wins can

- Provide evidence that sacrifices are worth it;
- Reward change agents with a pat on the back;
- Help to fine-tune vision and strategies;
- Undermine cynics and self-serving resisters;
- Keep bosses on board;
- Build momentum (Kotter, 2012, p.122).

The first short-term win that Lejeune instituted was a comprehensive physical fitness regimen. Lejeune provides a detailed explanation of his ideology by suggesting that

> The physical condition of troops has a great influence on their morale. Men whose bodies are untrained physically, who are soft from leading sedentary lives, are unable to stand the strain and stress of long marches and active campaigning. Their morale is rapidly lowered, and they soon become demoralized. The effect of physical training is exemplified in the case of Stonewall Jackson's division. In the fall campaign of '62, they made such long marches with so few stragglers that they were called the "Foot Cavalry." General Dick Taylor, who commanded one of the brigades, writes very interesting notes in his book entitled "Destruction and Reconstruction," telling how he trained his brigade to march. He said in '61 Jackson's division marched very poorly. It was composed largely of men who were brought up in the country and who were accustomed to ride on horse-back, or were city men who were accustomed to riding in carriages. Taylor took his brigade and practiced it in marching during the winter of '61

and '62, so in the spring of '63 his brigade marched so well that it was adopted by Jackson as an example for the whole division. The whole division was practiced in marching with the wonderful results that history tells us about. The morale of that division as we know was very high; perhaps the physical condition of the men had a great effect on it. (Lejeune, 2016, p. 81)

During his tenure as the AEF 2nd Division Commanding General, he experienced the firsthand effects of an athletic policy under General Pershing. As he recalled, "Football and baseball leagues were organized, and the rivalry and excitement caused by the games were intense, thousands of men being transported by motor trucks to witness games. To accommodate them great stands were constructed in every division area. Teams of boxers, too, travelled from place to place, and the manly art taught to thousands of men (Lejeune, 1930, Loc 5880). It is perhaps this wartime exposure that inspired him to embrace a comprehensive athletic policy and athletic activity, especially in connection with football and baseball (Lejeune, 1930, Loc 6287). This gesture of instilling physical fitness into the culture was Lejeune's attempt to enact the broken windows theory that existed in the mind-set of Marines.

REACH 10,000 REPS AND SETS
Malcolm Gladwell in his book *Outliers* asserted that 10,000 hours of practice is required to achieve the level of mastery associated with being a world-class expert—in anything. Without being exposed to the science of success, Lejeune principally made Gladwell's case as he endeavored to transform the culture of professionalism. Namely, the 13th Commandant argued that

Troops whose professional or military training has been neglected, and who are unskilled in the profession of arms, finding themselves unable to cope on equal terms with a highly trained enemy force of equal numbers, have their morale lowered, and it becomes increasingly difficult to obtain results with such troops until and unless they shall have received the careful training and instruction which all troops should have before being thrown into battle. There are many instances in history of the failure of untrained troops. They are particularly liable to panic. I think in our own history the most notable example is the Battle of Bull Run, where the Union Army became panic-stricken in the afternoon of the battle and broke and fled to Washington. General Grant tells us in his memoirs of a regiment in Illinois which was badly officered. Reports came into the governor's office of the depredations of troops. They seem to have committed atrocities all around southern Illinois, murders, robberies, drunkenness, everything of the kind. The governor turned to General Grant, and said, "What are we going to do?" Grant said, "Give me command of the regiment and I can train them." He was appointed colonel and took command of this regiment, instructed the officers, trained the men, worked them about eight hours a day, and in a few months, it was the best regiment of the Illinois troops. (Lejeune, 2016, p. 81)

When Lejeune took charge of the Corps, he understood the correlation between professionalism and winning. To this end, various institutes to train and educate the force were constructed on the ground of Quantico, Virginia. Additionally, this leader insisted that selected officers would annually attend Navy War Colleges, the

Army school of warfighting, and other technical schools. Moreover, Lejeune advocated for practical military training, and thus he revitalized pistol practice Expeditionary Force maneuvers. This march to reach 10,000 hours of reps and sets was an endeavor to mitigate panic, elevate morale, and guarantee a lethal force would be prepared to fight when the moment called.

INFUSE SPIRITUAL FITNESS

Lejeune utilized one of the most undervalued and marginalized aspects of warfighting to transform the Corps. More specifically, this top leader of the Marines employed the tenets of spiritual fitness to cultivate transformation. To illustrate, Lejeune believed that, "Esprit de corps and morale are kindred subjects; in fact, some writers consider them as synonymous. This, however, is not the case, as esprit de corps is only one of the factors which goes to constitute morale. Morale is three-fold—physical, mental or professional, and spiritual" (Lejeune, 2016, p. 81). At this point, a conversation has been offered on the physical (i.e., garbage can and the broken window theory) and the professional (i.e., reach 10,000 reps and sets), so now let's turn the attention of the reader to the spiritual. As Gabe observed his men in battle during WWI, he concluded that

> There is no substitute for the spiritual in war. Miracles must be wrought if victories are to be won, and to work miracles men's hearts must be afire with self-sacrificing love for each other, for their units, for their division, and for their country. If each man knows that all the officers and men in his division are animated with the same fiery zeal as he himself feels, unquenchable courage and unconquerable determination crush out fear and death becomes preferable to defeat dishonor. Fortunate indeed is the leader who commands such

men, and it is his most sacred duty to purify his own soul and to cast out from it all unworthy motives, for men are quick to detect pretense or insincerity in the leaders, and worse than useless as a leader is the man in whom they find evidences of hypocrisy or undue timidity, or whose acts do not square with his words. (Lejeune, 1930, Loc 4146)

Figure 6 The Pillars of Spiritual Fitness

From the above quote, as well as other writings of Lejeune, one can formulate a working definition for *spirituality*. Namely, this construct can be defined as the irreplaceable higher force that ignites the warriors to act out of self-sacrificing love, other-centeredness, to crush fear, and to constantly purify their soul from unworthy motives as they execute their purposes. From the perspective of the 13th Commandant, spirituality has four pillars that enable a warrior to effectively navigate through the fog of war.

Military Vices	Description
Cat 1—No discipline of the body (15%)	Vices that include substance abuse
Cat 2—Longings of the eyes (30%)	Vices that revolve around sexual misconduct
Cat 3—Hubris trappings of command (55%)	Vices that revolve around arrogant decisions

TABLE 3 MILITARY VICES

SELF-AWARENESS

As depicted in Figure 6, the first pillar of spirituality is self-awareness. It can be argued that self-awareness sparked by spirituality can illuminate a warrior's vices as well as their virtues. Regarding vices, Lejeune nested spirituality with the term *afire*. Fire brings light to dark places and can even purge away that which is not healthy. A cursory review of current military affairs suggests that there are three major vices that entangle senior leaders. Abstracting from the research of the Associated Press on why senior leaders were relieved of duty, there appeared to be three categories of vices (Baldor, 2013). The first category, as outlined in Table 3, is no discipline of the body. This cohort of senior military leaders were relieved of duty due to an inability to abstain from substance abuse. Though this class of leaders were talented, 15% found themselves depending on drugs, pills, or alcohol to navigate the pressures of command.

The second category of derailed commanders turned to sexually related misconduct to cope with the pressures of being at the top. Stated statistically, 30% of officers who were once positively screened to lead America's treasure in battle but had their aspirations foiled, were undone by the allure of illicit sex. The third grouping of commanding officers who were relieved of duty failed due to the hubris trappings of command; 55% of top military leaders were fired due to the creation of hostile work environments, toxic decision points, or the skewed ideology that it was all about them. From the perspective of Lejeune, a healthy form of spirituality could proactively check such vices before they catch root and grow into an organizational disease.

On the other side of the self-awareness coin is virtue. From the perspective of Aristotle, courage is the essence of not just happiness but life itself (Lee and Elliott-Lee, 2006). Building on Aristotle's assertion, Socrates contended that the source of courage is *thumos,* or spiritedness. For Lejeune there is a relationship between spirituality and a soldier's ability to acquire "unquenchable courage and unconquerable determination [to] crush out fear…[such that] death becomes preferable to defeat dishonor." A review of recent military historical events can provide evidence where spirituality was indeed an antecedent of a courageous act. Buford's (2018) research demonstrated the role that spiritual fitness played in the battlefield; courage of the likes of Hugh Thompson at My Lai, Colin Powell as a top statesman, and William Kyle Carpenter at Helmand Province, Afghanistan to name a few. Though not an exhaustive list of courageous warriors, such personalities have publicly acknowledged how *thumos* illuminated their courage.

AN ETHICAL VOICE

The second pillar of spiritual fitness is an ethical voice. Lejeune's rhetoric of spirituality purifying one's soul to check unworthy motives implies that one's morality can indeed be the difference maker on the battlefield. This assertion is largely predicated upon the 13th Commandant's experience in the first Great War. Namely, Lejeune observed that, "the spiritual needs of the men were ministered to on a vast scale. Literally hundreds of religious services were held weekly, and the best obtainable speakers were engaged in the great campaign to elevate the men morally and spiritually" (Lejeune, 1930, Loc 5892). When a warrior is spiritually fit, they have a greater propensity to speak up and to engage because it is the right thing to do. A modern-day example of this reality can be found in the actions of Dakota Meyer at Kunar Province, Afghanistan. When Meyer's fellow Marines were being ambushed and the chain of command refused aid, Dakota took charge. He mounted a gun-truck and retrieved his comrades in arms with total disregard for his own life. During a six-hour battle with a fellow Marine driving, they went in and out of the battle numerous times. Though he was properly trained as a Marine, it can be argued that the ultimate source of Meyer's ethical power flowed from his spirituality (Meyer and West, 2012, Loc 3250). This fact is perhaps the very reason Lejeune encouraged his officers "to train and cultivate the bodies, the minds and the spirit of our men" (Lejeune, 1920).

SPIRITUAL RESILIENCY

The third pillar upon Lejeune's spiritual fitness model is resiliency. Wick (2015, Loc 88) contends that spiritual resiliency is not simply about recovering from adversity. It is about bouncing back in a way that a deeper knowledge of spirituality and self may result....It is the resolve to never quit. Once again, Gabe's firsthand experiences and observations of war cultivated this firm conviction that spirituality can be an incredible overcoming tool. More specifically, Lejeune believed that, "it is indeed true in war the spiritual is to the material as three or even four to one" (Lejeune, 1930, Loc 4157). During a lecture to the Army General Staff College on 18 January 1921, he clarified the meaning of this statement:

High spirit, could defeat an army of low morale, and necessarily low spirit, which was three times as strong in numbers. A study of history shows that this has happened over and over again. In fact, small forces have defeated armies much greater than three times their size. (Lejeune, 2016, p. 82)

If one were to accept the proposition that in war the spiritual is to the material as three or even four to one, then one must also concede to the plausibility that the spiritual can help to overcome personal and internal battles like post-traumatic stress, moral injury, grief, and a plethora of other life challenges. Though the empirical research on this topic is rapidly emerging, the ensuing historical case provides further evidence of its positive impact.

In October 1963, LT James N. Rowe and two other soldiers were heading to their base camp Tan Phu in An Xuyon Province when they were ambushed by the NLF fighters, blindfolded, and taken into captivity at a hidden prison. After five years of failed escape attempts, Rowe finally succeeded to elude his captors. In an interview by the *Army Digest*, he was asked how he was able to survive such conditions for so long. "I had good mental discipline, and my faith in God strongly motivated me to live…I was a Protestant until I received spiritual training at West Point and this training allowed me to be mentally strong….West Point taught me that there is nothing materialistic you can grasp, and there are times when you have no place to turn except your spirituality." (Rowe, Pitzer and Versace, 1969, p. 4)

An examination of LT James Rowe's story is a shining military example that spiritual resiliency can infuse a person with purpose, optimism, and persevering grit.

INSPIRATION

The final pillar that warrants consideration is inspiration. The Latin translation of this term: *in-* means "to infuse," and *spirare* means "breath of life (spirit)." Thus, *inspiration* is the act of exciting, influencing, or arousing another into action. Such a definition is the very essence of leadership. From Lejeune's (2016, p. 82) perspective, "the spirit—is more or less an unknown field to all of us and a field which it is very difficult for us to comprehend by the exercise of our mental faculties. Logic and reasoning play but a small part of it. Education assists but little. It's a matter of dealing with the emotions, the spirit, the souls of the troops. A man successful in this realm is a great leader, and the qualities necessary to make him successful are known as the qualities of leadership." Thus, to bring the best out of a team, an influencer must master the art and science of the spirit.

The average leader overlooks the role of the spirit due to the difficulty of comprehending it fully. This unfortunate oversight limits the abilities of the leader as well as the led. When one disregards the spirit, courage cannot operate at an optimum level because the key element of courage is *thumos,* or spiritedness. When the spirit is marginalized, one's moral compass becomes skewed. When the spirit is driven out of the fiber of an organization, the esprit de corps (spirit of the body) declines. This, however, was not the case for the 13th Commandant. This leader became the greatest leatherneck of all time due to his ability to navigate and incorporate into the Corps the irreplaceable higher force that ignites afire the being of a warrior to walk out self-sacrificing love, other-centeredness, to crush fear, and to constantly purify one's soul from unworthy motives as they execute their purposes. Such operationalization of spirituality sets the conditions to explore the final element of the G.R.I.T. model.

TRANSPARENTLY GO THE EXTRA MILE

With the questions of relevancy surfacing, organizational morale declining, and new fiscal constraints being imposed, LtGen Lejeune knew he had to engage. And engage he did, in a transparent, visible, and beyond-the-call-of-duty manner. What was at the heart of this campaign? One can argue that this top leader of Marines endeavored to build trust in the hearts and minds of the American public. Long before the theory was presented in the bestseller, Lejeune employed some of Covey's (2006) principles of trust to accomplish the task—confront reality, get better, and deliver results transparently. This change-agent clearly understood the difficult terrain before him and confronted it with intentionality. Lejeune reflects:

> When I assumed the duties of Commandant, demobilization had been completed and the entire Corps was suffering from the consequent let-down which invariably follows the return of a military organization to peacetime conditions. Nearly all of the splendid men who had enlisted for the period of the emergency had resumed their civil occupations; many war-time officers had separated themselves from the service; wholesale demotions in rank had taken place; recruiting was slow; the number of enlisted men being only about 15,000, which was altogether insufficient to perform the important duties assigned to the Corps; there was much unrest among the officers owing to their uncertain status; and the lavish expenditures incident to war were to great extent still prevalent. (Lejeune, 1930, Loc 6244)

Though there are no public records of the initial private planning meetings of his administration, one can surmise by the above quote that he leaned in with opened eyes and delivered results.

POSITIVE TONE

As Lejeune mused upon the ugly truth, this influencer used the desk of the commandant to strike a positive tone and to send a clear message in two ways. As mentioned before, first he adopted as the guiding principle for his administration the rule that the good of the Corps, combined with the just treatment of all officers and men, was paramount and, therefore, took precedence over all other considerations. The practice of this principle precluded the exercise of favoritism (Lejeune, 1930, Loc 6258). Thus, this simple but profound act of positivity for the good of the Corps created an atmosphere of trust and confidence. Such a climate, it should be noted, successfully enabled silos (i.e., Naval Academy graduates, Bushwhackers, and WWI veterans) to move from operating from the toxic stage of cliques to creative collaboration for the country. Moreover, inspection of Lejeune's writing campaign to the fleet would reveal reinforcing positive language and tone. Namely, often this leader would conclude his correspondences in a spirit of optimism to all hands and without partiality.

When disrupters endeavored to undermine the position of the good of the Corps, Lejeune would not stoop to their level. On the contrary, it became a rule for the 13th Commandant

> Never to reprimand an enlisted man, or to censure an officer in the presence of his men. How could a Division Commander correct conditions among 28,000 men by shouting at an individual who might perhaps have his coat unbuttoned, or have on rubber boots under forbidden circumstance; or how could

junior officers retain the respect of their men if scathingly rebuked in their presence? Personally, I preferred to see the looks of affection in the eyes of the men when I went about them than to know that they feared and dreaded my visits. Kindness and justice combined with severe punishment of serious offenders will, I believe, result in a higher state of discipline than can be produced by constant nagging and by unduly harsh punishments for petty offenses. (Lejeune, 1930, Loc 4157)

Even in the face of friction points, Lejeune instinctively understood the science that positivity has on productivity. That is, when followers know that leaders demonstrate care and convey such attention in a fair as well as positive manner, it increases organizational trust, morale, and productivity (Zak, 2017).

PUBLIC IMPRESSION MANAGEMENT

Gabe pushed the Corps to transparently go the extra mile with public impression management. McShan and Glinow (2013, Loc 9131) explain that impression management is the practice of actively shaping public images for the purposes of advancing a cause, brand or an entity. In the face of the whispers of relevancy, Lejeune took his fight directly to the American public in several innovative ways. First, this influencer understood the value of searching for opportunities amid opposition. The domestic hostility manifested itself in the form of mail robberies. During 1920s there were 36 major thefts that amounted in a loss of $6,300,000. In collaboration with the government, the 13th Commandant gave the order to have the Marines ride the trains. During a yearlong mission with such a task force, only one robbery was attempted but failed (Norton, 2008). Second, Lejeune pivoted to the hub of entertainment for help. Namely, Gabe cultivated a friendship with a producer and co-founder of Metro-Goldwyn-Mayer studios (MGM). From this platform a silent film called *Tell It to the Marines* was produced. This film, featuring Lon Cheney Sr., was a smashing hit that later opened the door for other similar productions (i.e., *The Fighting Marine* and *What Price Glory*). While traveling, Lejeune wrote to his friend Smedley Butler that, "There were three Marine Corps moving picture films being exhibited in Boston, I was told, all playing to crowed houses" (Norton, 2008).

Lejeune wasn't satisfied with crowed houses in movie theaters. Though it helped to move the public impression management needle, he knew he needed to change the perception of political leaders too. To this end, he put Quantico Base on the map by building an athletic field, forming competitive football teams, and inviting top influencers to observe. Moreover, Gabe gave the order to the Marines to conduct Civil War reenactments. The execution of this directive typically began with a march from Marine Corps Base Quantico to the various battlegrounds. Once in position, key political decision makers, to occasionally include the President of the United States, would observe a display of military might (Norton, 2008).

But perhaps Lejeune's most effective public impression management tool were the Marines themselves. Accordingly, he would often remind the forces of this fact in letters like the following.

> In the first place, I want each of you to feel that the Commandant of the Corps is your friend and that he earnestly desires that you should realize this. At the same time, it is his duty to the Government and to the Marine Corps to exact a high standard of conduct, a strict performance of duty, and a rigid compliance with orders on the part of all the

officers....The prestige of the Marine Corps depends greatly on the appearance of its officers and men. Officers should adhere closely to the uniform regulations, and be exceedingly careful to be neatly and tidily dressed, and to carry themselves in a military manner. They should observe the appearance of the men while on liberty, and should endeavor to instill into their minds the importance of neatness, smartness and soldierly bearing....You are the permanent part of the Marine Corps, and the efficiency, the good name, and the esprit of the Corps are in your hands. You can make or mar it. (Lejeune, 1922)

Thus, he put the onus on the Marines to transform public thinking by choosing to make it, not mar the legacy of the past with substandard conduct on and off duty.

PROPHETIC ORGANIZATIONAL RESTRUCTURE

In the book *The Structure of Scientific Revolutions,* Kuhn makes the case that when current models no longer adequately explain a phenomenon, a paradigm shift becomes the order of the day (Kuhn, 1996). To this end, Lejeune's collective contributions to the Corps suggest that he understood that a modification to structure could potentially be healthy for the team if handled prudently. The research indicates that when a firm does undergo a restructure, it typically engenders a dualist response. According to Jong et al. (2016), for the people at the top who have status, their well-being remains high. Whereas those outside the status circle have a propensity to digress onto a negative pathway due to the ambiguity affiliated with new roles and responsibilities. As such, the literature suggests that influencers can mitigate the dark side of restructures by acquainting oneself with the principles of change management, clearly codifying roles as well as responsibilities, and training the team to the new standard.

This guidance is exactly what Lejeune personified as he introduced prophetic organizational restructure into the Corps. The term *prophetic* is used intentionally due to the far-reaching impact of Gabe's decision into the future. Bartlett (1991, p. 148) submits that

> Immediately upon taking the reins of the Corps on 30 June 1920, Lejeune began a major reorganization of Headquarters Marine Corps so as to alter its traditional functions. The act of 11 July 1798 authorized the appointment of additional officers to assist the commandant in his duties. Legislation on 3 March 1903 added to the number of assistants and increased the rank of some of them. The passage of significant personnel legislation during World War One resulted in the promotion of the commandant's principal assistants—adjutant and inspector, quartermaster, and paymaster—to brigadier general. Not surprisingly, by the time Lejeune became the thirteenth commandant, the incumbents on the staff had established their own fiefs.

In light of the subkingdoms and the power grabbing of the brigadier generals, Lejeune restructured the headquarters and clarified expectations. The ultimate intent of this maneuver was to actualize one of his top priorities—the efficiency of the Corps. The secondary effect was to create a "staff that responded to direction from his office to the demands and requirements of the Marine Corps at large" (Bartlett, 1991, p. 148).

PIONEER FISCAL RESPONSIBILITY

The fourth way that Lejeune transparently went the extra mile was fiscally. To recap, Congress was driving the nation back to a state of "normalcy." This endeavor called for each branch to scale back on requirements, and the Corps was not immune. Throughout his commandancy, the top Marine would feverishly push back on deeper cuts and would caution that

> To reduce the Corps would be highly detrimental to its morale and efficiency. All Marines know that the Corps is now too small and consequently overworked, and they would feel that any further reduction of its strength was an indication that those in authority did not regard very highly its value to the nation. (Bartlett, 1991, p. 162)

Upon providing his best military advice on the matter, he would demonstrate his allegiance and employ a principle that stands to this day. Krulak (1984, Loc 4415) best captured this code when he wrote, "it was an instinct of austerity that inspired Commandant Lejeune, after World War I, to establish a policy of returning, each year, to the Treasury, a part of the Marine Corps appropriation." This small but profound gesture helped to push back on negative narratives as well as to build trust in the leadership of this warfighting organization.

PROTECT THE NATION

At the end of the day, Lejeune understood the chief function of the Corps. Though navigating the rugged terrain of morale, fiscal concerns, and questions of relevancy were paramount, he kept the main thing the main thing—making Marines, winning battles, and returning Marines back to society as better citizens. In the context of an international armistice, Lejeune coined a motto that would focus the Corps as well as the nation. This slogan, debatably, was given life on 12 January 1922 while he addressed officers at Quantico. During that speech, he signaled to this crowd and by extension the nation, "in times of peace, prepare for war!" This rallying cry pushed Lejeune's Corps to train to the standards of its legacy. Asprey (1962) best captures the 13th Commandant's ideology when he reminded Marines that they exist "to support the United States Fleet, and to aid the Navy in carrying out that part of the policy of the government which had been or may be assigned to it." Moreover, "the major war mission of the Marine Corps…is to support the Fleet by supplying it with a highly trained fully equipped expeditionary force for…the seizure and defense of temporary or advanced naval bases in the theatre of operations." Such a message undoubtedly resonated with the top leadership, the Corps, as well as the nation. Why? Because it spoke to the dominant need of Americans—security. According to theory, when people feel protected, their confidence in such an entity increases.

CONCLUSION

As various organizations endeavor to move the needle and find the competitive edge in the 21st century, it would serve them well to employ John A. Lejeune's G.R.I.T. model, which is to garbage-can the broken window theory, reach 10,000 reps and sets, infuse spiritual fitness, and transparently go the extra mile. Following such a model, it is reasonable to conclude that significance will be the by-product and a healthier entity will emerge. To this end, servants such as Lejeune naturally display their G.R.I.T. not for personal gain, but for the sake of the institution.

Kneecap to Kneecap Discussion

Virtually every sea service in the 21st century is asserting that in the next great campaign, warriors will "have to fight to get to the fight." This expression points toward the possible challenges that sea services may encounter before an engagement. With this assertion in mind, think about, discuss, and wrestle with the following.

1. If you were in charge of an organization that was being confronted with questions of relevancy, morale, and fiscal constraints, how would you as leader prepare yourself to engage?

2. Robert Greenleaf's second aspect of his "best test" question revolves around the health question of those under your leadership. While considering this, how would you rate the current health of your team? What do you need to do to improve?

3. In your own words, describe the broken window theory and share a time when you witnessed a leader proactively confront this in a healthy way. Outline some practical ways you can better get at this principle with your own team today.

4. Which one of the spiritual fitness pillars resonates the most with you and why?

5. How much G.R.I.T. on a scale of 1 to 5 (5 being the best) does your organization have today, and what can you do to improve upon it?

Overseas Review, 1919.

CHAPTER FIVE

BEYOND PERFUNCTORY LEARNING

"To accomplish this task successfully a constant effort must be made by all officers to fill each day with useful and interesting instructions and wholesome recreation for the men. This effort must be intelligent and not perfunctory, the object being not only to eliminate idleness, but to train and cultivate the bodies, the minds, and the spirit of our men."

-John A. Lejeune

The third question that a researcher must analyze to determine whether or not a person is a servant-leader is, Do the served become wiser? In an endeavor to wrestle with this aspect of the discussion, the reader's attention will be focused upon the characteristics of the 21st-century Marine while concurrently reviewing Lejeune's ideology on learning. To frame the conversation, it should be noted that wisdom can be defined as the ability to discern the appropriate course of action to be taken in a given situation at the appropriate time. Such a definition can be an invaluable commodity in today's information age.

Scholars have suggested that the genesis of the information age officially started in the 1970s. It was during this timeframe that the Department of Defense conceptualized and implemented the internet as a strategic tool of engagement. Not only did this gesture open the door of creative possibilities in other ventures, it also made the world flat and the quest for information supreme. Such a hunt motivated the likes of Bill Gates to cast a simple but provocative vision, "A computer on every desk, in every home, running Microsoft software." Such a focus coupled with the barrage of other media, smart phones, and thirst for real-time news has transformed the American way of life.

Instead of relying upon old-fashioned virtues like arduous work, institutions of faith, and traditional family structures to forge value-centric wisdom like that of the industrialized age, the tenet of this generation tends to be forged by google, smart phones, texting, technology, and other digital outlets. An unattended effect, however, of this trend is the creation of a new set of philosophies. The Pew Research Center illuminates this point in a study by asserting that Millennials "are relatively unattached to organized politics and religion, linked by social media, burdened by debt, distrustful of people, in no rush to marry—and optimistic about the future" (Pew Research, 2014). This Millennial ethos of being unattached to traditional norms, distrustful of others, yet linked by social media, may present a degree of tension if it is not handled with prudence.

This tension may manifest itself in the life of the Millennial Marine when it's time to render traditional military courtesies. In other words, if a person has the natural propensity to be distrustful of other people, then one shouldn't be too surprised if a Marine is not enthused to exercise instantaneous obedience to orders. Cognitive dissonance may very well be the order of the day for a Marine to be told to exercise good judgment and not post coarse content about themselves on social media. Such an assertion would not only be a foreign concept, but it may go against their core values, as this has been a way of life from infancy. Additionally, it may be an oxymoron for warriors of the information age to sustain the transformation when the information being conveyed is not delivered in an understandable manner. Considering this tension, the questions become, Did Lejeune make the Corps wiser, how specifically did Lejeune impart wisdom into the Marines of his era, and can such pedagogy be applicable today?

A plausible answer to the above questions may reside within the very behavior of the information-age warrior. Namely, despite being unattached and distrustful of others, it should be noted that the 21st-century Marine willingly volunteered to stand on those yellow footprints at boot camp. Since they decided to join the Marine Corp, could it be that they long to be transformed to the Marine's way of life, or is it safer to assume that this generation will transform the Corps? The mere fact that this chapter, as well as others, are being written may imply that a more reasonable answer lays somewhere in the middle. This moment calls for a relevant model that will preserve history yet embrace the future. As such, the ensuing dialogue will attempt to answer the questions of this chapter and present a revitalized training curriculum to help information-age warriors embrace the Marine Corps way and to help the Marine Corps to embrace this new era.

INTELLIGENT & NOT PERFUNCTORY

Though Millennials are unattached, distrustful of others, and linked by social media, they made a choice to join the Marine Corps and are optimistic about the future. This seed of hopefulness can either flourish into the next generation of ethical warfighters or simply wither away. The determining factor of a Marine's future hinges largely upon the leader's ability to properly train and educate them. Lejeune underscored this mandate when he wrote

> The relation between officers and enlisted men should in no sense be that of superior and inferior, not that of master and servant, but rather that of *teacher and scholar*. In fact, it should partake of the nature of the relation between father and son, to the extent that officers, especially commanders, are responsible for the physical, mental, and moral welfare, as well as the discipline and military training of the men under their command who are serving the Nation in the Marine Corps. The recognition of this responsibility on the part of officers is vital to the well-being of the Marine Corps. It is especially so for the reason that so large a proportion of the men enlisting are under 21 years of age. These men are in the formative period of their lives and officers owe it to them, to their parents, and to the Nation, that when discharged from the service they should be far better men physically, mentally

and morally than they were when they enlisted. To accomplish this task successfully a constant effort must be made by all officers to fill each day with useful and interesting instructions and wholesome recreation for the men. This effort must be *intelligent and not perfunctory*, the object being not only to eliminate idleness, but to train and cultivate the bodies, the minds, and the spirit of our men [emphasis mine]. (Lejeune, 1920)

Three key points can be abstracted from Lejeune's Marine Corps Order No. 29, *Relations between Officers and Men*. First, the language back then reflected the political realities of the 1920s; women were not yet part of the ranks. But for this publication, it should be noted that terms like *men* and *father* can be used interchangeably with *women* and *mother* (a more detailed discussion on this topic will happen in Chapter Six). Secondly, Lejeune places a mandate on officers, especially commanders, to become an educator. This effort, thirdly, to educate America's treasure, particularly in their formative years, should have the appropriate technique and delivery. Namely, officers should not facilitate learning from a position of superiority, but rather one's deliberation should be parental or that of a teacher and scholar. Moreover, such an effort should be clever and not have the feeling of yet another *check-the-box* training. On the contrary, Lejeune contended that the end goal is to develop the whole Marine—mind, body, and spirit.

The possible problem with the above mandate, however, is that Marine commanders and officers are primarily trained in the art of warfighting and not necessarily on the science of adult education. In other words, leaders are given the responsibility of conducting Professional Military Education (PME) in the command but were not given the tools and the wisdom to do it more efficiently. Because of this institutional blind spot, the PME's take on more of a perfunctory or *check-the-box* task. Considering this assertion, perhaps it would be a logical gesture to repackage Lejeune's *teacher and scholar* with a learning theory designed to transform an information-age citizen into a 21st-Century Marine?

PEOPLE REMEMBER
10% of what we READ------------->
20% of what we HEAR------------->   <---- Passive or Perfunctory Learning
30% of what we SEE---------------->
50% of what we SEE & HEAR---->   <---- Active or Intelligent Learning
70% of what we SAY --------------->
90% of what we SAY & DO------->

THE 21ST CENTURY TEACHER & SCHOLAR MODEL

Dale's Learning Cone could possibly serve as a tool to assure, in the sentiments of Lejeune, that command learning remains *intelligent and not perfunctory.* As depicted in Figure 7, the retention of knowledge fluctuates with the various methods of scholarship. For example, Cone contends that learners remember only 10% of what they read, and 20% of information received from a typical lecture. This percentage increases to 30% when an instructor strategically incorporates visual aids like figures, charts, and other static displays. These forms of learning platforms at best foster passive learning. Passive learning can be defined as a

> Type of learning in which it is assumed that the students will enter the course which they want to study with open minds, which are like empty vessels or sponges, and the teachers will

merely fill the minds of the students with knowledge. (Heath, 2014)

Though the passive approach is easier for the teacher and takes less effort, it can be costly as well as ineffective. That is, the overall body of knowledge indicates that students don't grow in this way. They are reluctant to ask clarifying questions and become bored.

The other side of the passive learning construct is Cone's description of active learning. Active learning "involves the learning by being engaged in the instructional process by means of such activities as exploring, analyzing, communicating, creating, reflecting, or actually using new information or experiences" (Heath, 2014). As outlined in Figure 7, 50% of information is retained when a learner engages with props such as videos and guided discussion. Seventy percent of instruction resonates when students teach back sessions or are encouraged to analyze problems in small groups. Ninety percent of instructional data is received and retained when the student can demonstrate the information. All in all, if this warfighting organization is to replicate Lejeune's *Teacher & Scholar* model in today's context, then it would behoove influencers to become more cognizant of the discipline of adult education. For, at the end of the day, this very method could be the difference between battlefield victory or blunder.

L.E.A.P. INTO THE FUTURE

In an endeavor to impart wisdom into the mind, body, and spirit of the next generation of warfighters, organizations are encouraged to take a L.E.A.P. into the future. Such a model can be referred to as the Lejeune Ethical Arming Project (L.E.A.P.). L.E.A.P. fuses the active side of Cone's learning ideal with Lejeune's counsel to embrace a *teacher and scholar* style of facilitation as opposed to a knife-hand approach that cultivates a *superior and inferior* environment. Moreover, this two- to three-block seminar can utilize proven historical traits to help the 21st-century warrior to be molded afresh into the Marine way of life. The intent of the following curriculum is not to be prescriptive, due to the respective nuances of each command. On the contrary, the ensuing framework is a possible description of a program of study to help train and cultivate the mind, body, and spirit of a Marine.

LOCATION

When possible, it is recommended to conduct L.E.A.P. at a central location in civilian attire. This gesture can help to establish a teacher and scholar training atmosphere as well as to create an atmosphere of academic learning. Moreover, the attendance should not exceed 50 people in each class and should be populated by rank. The ideology behind the class capacity is undergirded by theory. That is, research shows that learning decreases drastically when the class is greater than fifty. Additionally, due to the military-bearing aspect, the makeup of the class should be rank-centric. This move could possibly help to cultivate a transparent and confidential discussion about some difficult topics.

BLOCK ONE: ANCHORING (THE TACTICAL VERSION)

The Case Study: After a few years of working odd jobs in his hometown, 21-year-old Jamie decides that there is more to life than working for minimum wages and hanging out with friends that are content doing nothing with their lives. Though he deeply desired to go to college, his parents just could not afford it. As a result of being raised in a lower middle-class section of America, Jamie had plenty of opportunities to engage in more mischief. Though his family were devoted Republicans and Evangelical Christians, Jamie didn't share his family's ideology. In fact, most of his pastime is spent on social media, working on cars, paying off credit cards, and working out. As fate would have it, he bumps into a Marine recruiter in uniform at the mall one day. A conversation emerged that made him recall that his grandfather served as a Marine, and he made the commitment to enlist. After all, this was his ticket out of his hometown. After a few weeks of boot camp, this recruit was really struggling. He struggled over the fact that he was away from home for the first time and surrounded by other people who were different from himself. He struggled internally and wasn't too sure of himself or the decision he made to become a Marine. He struggled around this guy named Drill Instructor who loved to call him out by name. The Drill Instructor, in so many words, instructed Jamie to fix himself, pull it together, or get out of his Marine Corps! The Drill Instructor had tried nearly every method to motivate this recruit to push beyond limitations to no avail. This recruit is sent to you to help him "find himself" and to "get himself together" before he is kicked out of boot camp.

The Facilitator: Whoever the command selects to facilitate the L.E.A.P. seminar should be thoroughly acquainted with adult learning as well as the teacher–scholar approach of training. While inviting the class to break off into 10 groups of five Marines, the facilitator will ask each group to select a spokesperson as they work through the case study to wrestle with the following assignment.

Resources: Position Post-it notepads and dry erase markers throughout the classroom.

Case Study Assignment (15 min): (1) While in small groups, come to a consensus whether you think Jamie will make it out of boot camp. Be sure to defend your answer with examples. (2) Outline the five reasons why some Marines struggle and are dismissed from training. (3) If this recruit were brought to you by the Drill Instructor to help him "find himself" and "get himself together," devise a collective plan as a group to aid this Recruit to overcome.

Case Study Debriefing (15 min): Randomly ask a group to debrief their assignments. Instead of this being a mechanical exercise, feel free to ask further probing questions to stimulate thought and group discussion. The facilitator should use their best judgment to encourage a respectful discussion while at the same time raising questions about the mind, body, and spirit without lecturing. Once each group has completed teaching back, be sure to affirm all responses. This ice breaker can set the stage to conduct an inclusive conversation about hard topics.

*At the completion of the teach-back session, the facilitator can locate appropriate videos, exercises, and implement guided discussion based on the following constructs.

Anchor Question 1: What does spiritual fitness mean to you and can this help a Marine to overcome life challenges?

Anchor Question 2: (While displaying General Lejeune's assertion that there is no substitute for the spiritual in warfare) What did General Lejeune mean by this quote?

Anchor Question 3: Give examples of a Marine displaying self-sacrificing love and explain how others can replicate this virtue.

Anchor Question 4: Other-centeredness is a leadership trait that propels a Marine not to ask, "What's in it for me?" but, "What's best for the rest?" Why do some people prefer a self-centered lifestyle as opposed to other-centeredness, and how can the virtue of other-centeredness be cultivated in us?

Anchor Question 5: Identify three courageous Marines and explain why they are courageous. How can Marines today learn to better crush fear and lead in the fog of war with moral clarity?

Anchor Question 6: What does it mean to seek self-improvement, and why is this important to warfighting?

Anchor Question 7: How can a Marine purify themselves from unworthy motives that can undermine their purpose, their family, and overall mission readiness?

BLOCK TWO:

THE CHARACTER OF THE CORPS

(THE TACTICAL VERSION)

The Case Study: (The facilitator begins this block of instruction by informing the class that Jamie has made it successfully through boot camp and now is facing a major ethical dilemma. After setting the stage, the facilitator will show a clip like "The Killings at the Canal.")

Resources: The usage of the turning point polling software is recommended. Once the software is uploaded, the following question can be displayed:

The Character of the Corps Question 1: In your honest opinion, what was the main contributor to this mishap?

    A. Blind Loyalty

    B. Leadership

    C. Combat Stress

    D. Something Else

Case Study Assignment (15 min): In small groups, (1) discuss your peers' votes, and be sure to explain the why behind the respective responses. (2) List the top five reasons why some Marines behave unethically and consequently are relieved of duty. (3) As a group, come to a consensus on how this ethical mishap can be mitigated in the future and be sure to explain how this impacts warfighting internationally.

Case Study Debriefing (15 min): Randomly ask a group to debrief their assignments. Instead of this being a mechanical exercise, feel free to ask further probing questions to stimulate thought and group discussion. The facilitator should use their best judgment to encourage a respectful discussion while at the same time raising questions about the *Character of the Corps* without lecturing. Once each group has completed teaching back, be sure to affirm all responses. This ice breaker can set the stage to conduct a more in-depth and inclusive conversation about the *Character of the Corps*.

*At the completion of the teach-back session, the facilitator can locate appropriate videos and exercises, and implement guided discussion based on the following constructs.

The Character of the Corps Question 2: What is knowledge, and why is it essential to warfighting?

The Character of the Corps Question 3: What is integrity, how does it strengthen, and why is it critical to the mission?

The Character of the Corps Question 4: How sound was the judgment of Jamie in the video? How does one develop good judgment on and off the battlefield? Can a leader recover from a poor judgment call—explain.

The Character of the Corps Question 5: What is decisiveness, and why does the Marine Corps value this as an important leadership trait?

BLOCK THREE: THE MARINE CORPS PROFESSION OF ARMS (THE TACTICAL VERSION)

The Case Study: (The facilitator begins this block of instruction by reminding the class that we live in the information age and technology has been with many of us since infancy. After setting the stage, the facilitator will display a snapshot of a solider taking a picture of herself hiding during colors. On the bottom of the snapshot, the solider essentially defends her position and states that saluting the flag is overrated.)

Resources: Locate this snapshot online and incorporate it into Power Point. Once this is displayed, use turning point software to upload the following question:

The Marine Corps Profession of Arms Question 1: In your honest opinion, should this soldier be reprimanded for posting this photo of herself on social media?

    A.   No – what's the big deal?

    B.   Yes – this discredits herself & the command

    C.   It depends

Case Study Assignment (15 min): In small groups, (1) discuss your peers' votes, and be sure to explain the why behind the respective responses. (2) List the top five reasons why some Marines get in trouble with social media. (3) As a group, come to a consensus if social media makes or mars the Profession of Arms.

Case Study Debriefing (15 min): Randomly ask a group to debrief their assignments. Instead of this being a mechanical exercise, feel free to ask further probing questions to stimulate thought and group discussion. The facilitator should use their best judgment to encourage a respectful discussion while at the same time raising questions about the *Profession of Arms* without lecturing. Once each group has completed teaching back, be sure to affirm all responses. This ice breaker can set the stage to conduct a more in-depth and inclusive conversation about the *Marine Corps Profession of Arms.*

*At the completion of the teach-back session, the facilitator can locate appropriate videos and exercises, and implement guided discussion based on the following constructs.

The Marine Corps Profession of Arms Question 2: What does it mean to be loyal to your country, the Corps, your chain of command, and your peers? Are there times that you must break this loyalty—explain.

The Marine Corps Profession of Arms Question 3: Partner with someone and tell them about the most dependable Marine that you know. Explain in detail why this person is this way, why you admire this person, and what you can learn from them?

The Marine Corps Profession of Arms Question 4: In small groups, recount a moment in the fog of war that a Marine displayed initiative. Be sure to define the term and explain what others can learn from them today.

The Marine Corps Profession of Arms Question 5: What did General Lejeune mean when he wrote in Order No. 1, "You are the permanent part of the Marine Corps, and the efficiency, the good name, and the esprit of the Corps are in your hands. You can make or mar it."

The Marine Corps Profession of Arms Question 6: What is justice, and why is it so important to warfighting?

The Marine Corps Profession of Arms Question 7: If you had to select one leadership trait to cultivate a strong Marine Corps

Profession of Arms, which word would you select and why? Loyalty, Dependability, Initiative, Bearing, or Justice

*The capstone assignment of L.E.A.P. is to charge each group to design a unique small unit training curriculum that includes *spiritual fitness* (anchor), the *Character of the Corps* (globe), and the *Marine Corps Profession of Arms* (eagle) to build resilient warriors. This project will be presented to class at the appointed time and will further help the student to internalize the findings of this study.

SOME EVIDENCE OF A WISER CORPS

Now that the question of imparting wisdom into this era of Marines has been addressed with the above model, let's briefly consider the inquiry, Did Lejeune make the Corps wiser? If in fact wisdom is the ability to discern the appropriate course of action to be taken in a given situation at the appropriate time, then one would have to conclude that under his leadership the Corps became more prudent. Bates (2014) would agree with this assertion by outlining the following achievements Lejeune left as evidence.

- Founded the Marine Corps Association and its magazine, the *Marine Corps Gazette.*

- Established the *Leatherneck* as a base newspaper in 1917 to tell the Marine Corps story. It became the *Leatherneck* magazine.

- Created via congressional act the Marine Corps League.

- Established the Marine Corps birthdate (10 November 1775).

- Created and conducted the first Marine Corps birthday celebration (Philadelphia, PA, 1923).

- Established the Marine Corps Institute for enlisted Marines.

- Established the Overseas Depot in World War I to train Marines for deployment to combat.

- Supported the assignment and establishment of the first female Marines (World War I).

- Drafted war plans in the 1920s (revised in the 1930s) for the conduct of an amphibious war in the Pacific against Japan.

- Maintained the Marine Corps as a positive force in readiness in the eyes of the American public.

- Believed strongly in and required academic education combined with professional training for all Marine officers.

- Started the creation of a Marine Corps amphibious force permanently attached to the east and west coast Navy fleets.

- Kept Marine Corps–Navy aviation within the Marine Corps and Navy.

- Established the genesis of the *Small Wars Manual* (finally published in 1940).

These examples of a wiser organization do not, regrettably, provide specific insights of Lejeune's pedagogy nor do other sources. Thus, a reasonable answer cannot be offered on how exactly the 13th Commandant employed his teacher–scholar model. One can infer, however, that his message of intelligent interactions did resonate in the fleet, and the leaders in the 1920s went beyond perfunctory learning. As the collision of values continues to unfold in the 21st-century warfighting organizations, perhaps it is time to revive the spirit of Lejeune's model for the sake of the republic.

Kneecap to Kneecap Discussion

1. In your opinion, does the military have a blind spot with regards to the delivery of learning? Please provide examples as you discuss this question.

2. While thinking about Cone's model of adult learning, which aspect is in operation the most in the military? Which aspect speaks the most to you and why?

3. Lejeune charged his officers to train and cultivate the bodies, the minds, and the spirit of the team with intelligent learning. Reflect back on your career and talk about a training that embraced this guidance. What made this a great period of instruction, and how can you replicate that now?

4. This chapter outlined a model to engage the 21st-century Marine: L.E.A.P. As an exercise, incorporate this model in your organization and reflect on the good, bad, and ugly realities of this approach.

5. Discuss why it is important for a leader to leave an organization wiser. In your discussion, provide examples of other leaders who have successfully modeled this trait today. What do you need to do to improve upon your ability to leave the led wiser?

 CHAPTER SIX

THE MISSING INGREDIENT

"Miracles must be wrought if victories are to be won, and to work miracles men's hearts must needs be afire with self-sacrificing love for each other, for their units, for their division, and for their country."

-John A. Lejeune

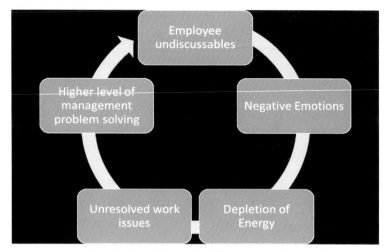

Figure 8 Ryan & Oestreich's The Negative Cost Cycle

The fourth question that a researcher needs to explore to understand wheather or not a person is a servant-leader is, Do the served become freer? To answer this inquiry, one must first understand the meaning of the word *freer*. Though Robert Greenleaf does not discuss the nuances of such a term, a working definition can be formulated by reverse engineering Ryan and Oestreich's (1998) research on fear in the workplace. As depicted in Figure 8, organizations that insert fear or indifference into the culture should not be surprised when they experience a high negative tax. The first symptom of such a climate is the existence of undiscussables. "An undiscussable is a problem or issue that someone hesitates to talk about with those who are essential to its resolution" (Loc 971). This inability to discuss the metaphorical elephant in the room is largely due to what happened to previous colleagues. In other words, when a coworker naively pointed out the warts of the firm, that person was either immediately fired or experienced retaliation.

This unfortunate norm creates a toxic environment. In such a space, the organizational citizens experience frustration, increased fear, anger, bitterness, cynicism, and resentment (Ryan and Oestreich, 1998). This toxic range of negative emotions often manifest in the depletion of energy. Once followers run on empty, mistakes increase, and innovation comes to a screeching halt. This results in unresolved work issues, and the team fails to seize upon golden opportunities. The sum of this entire cycle results in higher levels of management engagement and increased bureaucracy. Why? Because most organizational citizens are incapacitated by Ryan and Oestreich's (1998) notion of fear in the workforce. To this end, being freer (in terms of this book) can be defined as liberation from the negative taxes affiliated with the fear or indifference caused by an influencer.

A HARDER LOOK AT THE RELATION BETWEEN

It can be argued that the ultimate key to free workers from the tyranny of a toxic climate can be found in an intangible space. Lejeune describes this location as "the relation between." He states that

> The relation between officers and enlisted men should in no sense be that of *superior* and *inferior* not that of *master* and *servant*, but rather that of *teacher and scholar*. In fact, it should partake of the nature of the relation between *father* and *son*, to the extent that officers, especially commanders, are responsible for the physical, mental, and moral welfare, as well as the discipline and military training of the men under their command who are serving the Nation in the Marine Corps. The recognition of this responsibility on the part of officers is vital to the well-being of the Marine Corps. It is especially so for the reason that so large a proportion of the men enlisting are under 21 years of age. These men are in the

formative period of their lives and officers owe it to them, to their parents, and to the Nation, that when discharged from the service they should be far better men physically, mentally and morally than they were when they enlisted. To accomplish this task successfully a constant effort must be made by all officers to fill each day with useful and interesting instructions and wholesome recreation for the men. This effort must be intelligent and not perfunctory, the object being not only to eliminate idleness, but to train and cultivate the bodies, the minds, and the spirit of our men [emphasis & bold mine]. (Lejeune, 1920)

A harder look at this famous quote begs the question, What exactly is this space between father and son? In the context of a healthy father and son relationship, such as the one John A. Lejeune had with his father Ovide Lejeune, this space can be referred to as love. In addition to doing the right thing, at the right time, and for the right reasons, this form of love manifests in six ways.

PHYSIOLOGICAL NEEDS

The first aspect of love that one can abstract from the relation between a father and son/daughter or mother and daughter/son is physiological. This form of parental love guarantees that basic needs such as shelter, water, and food are readily available. In the context of warfighting, Marines' leaders understand the sentiments of the book *Gates of Fire: An Epic Novel of the Battle of Thermopylae,* and their love causes them not to abide within their tent while the led bleed and die on the field. Nor does a leader dine while the led go hungry, or sleep while they stand at watch upon the wall. Moreover, this aspect of leaderly love does not command the led's loyalty through fear nor do they purchase it with gold; they earn love by the sweat on their own back and the pains they endure for the sake of the led.

PROTECTION

The second manifestation of leaderly love is a willingness to protect the led by any means necessary. Though a more detailed conversation about this topic will unfold in Chapter Ten, the reader should understand at this point that this form of care defies logic. It is akin to a child being accidentally pinned under a car and, upon recognizing such an ordeal, the parent finds supernatural strength to lift the car to free the child. It is that same selfless love that will shield the led from attacks, assume responsibility for the wrong of the team while giving credit to others for organizational successes, and would willingly jump on a literal or metaphorical grenade so that the led can live. It is this form of love that exists between father/mother and son/daughter that inspires the led to storm the gates of hell.

PURPOSEFUL BUILDING OF BELONGINGNESS

Considering the dangers and challenges affiliated with maturing in today's culture, leaderly love endeavors to purposefully build belongingness. In a recent study, Brown and colleagues wanted to understand the benefits of belonging. As part of the study, they asked participants to place their hands in icy water. What they discovered was very practical, yet profound. That is, when the participant had someone with them, they were empowered to endure the pain longer than if they did the task alone (Brown et al., 2003). To this end, leaderly love intentionally builds teams that depend upon each other. It is this connection or new family (i.e., brothers and sisters) that cultivates resiliency, which is a critical component of warfighting.

PREPARATION

The fourth aspect of leaderly love is preparation. It is at this place that the leaderly father or mother assumes the responsibility to train up the led in the way they should go with the hopes that when they mature, they will embrace such fundamental codes, particularly when challenges emerge. Lejeune would suggest that such preparation should not be done haphazardly but focused on "the physical, mental, and moral welfare" of the Marines. Moreover, such preparation should include "discipline and military training." It is this form of preparation that equips warriors to thrive in the fog of war, excel as well in garrison, and function as a productive citizen once they return to the ranks of society. In short, preparation is a manifestation of love.

POSITIONING FOLLOWERS TO THRIVE

The final component of leaderly love is positioning followers to thrive. In other words, due to knowledge an influencer observes from the led, an objective estimate can be framed. Within this leaderly estimate, a clear understanding can potentially be unearthed about the led's strengths as well as their limitations. Equipped with such a data point, leaderly love endeavors to place the led in positions that can accentuate their gifts and encourage personal growth. In the context of the military, this might mean the leader influences the system to strategically place the led on the bus and in the right seat for the health of the organization as well as the individuals they lead (Collins, 2001).

PROPORTIONATE DISCIPLINE

It was as if Lejeune understood the counsel of a wise king that once said in Proverbs 13:24, "He who spares his rod hates his son, but he who loves him disciplines him promptly." Though an adequate discussion on the nine dimensions of Lejeunian discipline has been offered in Chapter Three, it is important to emphasize at this point the leaderly love in which he engaged. More specifically, Lejeune best summarizes the spirit of proportionate discipline by stating that

> I made it a rule never to reprimand an enlisted man, or to censure an officer in the presence of his men. How a could a Division Commander correct conditions among 28,000 men by shouting at an individual who might perhaps have his coat unbuttoned, or have on rubber boots under forbidden circumstances; or how could junior officers retain the respect of their men if scathingly rebuked in the presence? Personally, I preferred to see the looks of affection in the eyes of the men when I went about among them than to know that they feared and dreaded my visits. Kindness and justice combined with severe punishment of serious offenders will, I believe, result in a higher state of discipline than can be produced by constant nagging and by unduly harsh punishments for petty offenses. (Lejeune, 1930, Loc 4157)

Thus, Lejeune was a champion of discipline because he loved the Marines. Like any good father, he understood that at times the led will still have a coat unbuttoned or the wrong shoes will occasionally be worn to formation. When, not if, that happens, leaderly love reprimands in private for the purposes of development and does not lead with nagging or fear.

THE IMPACT OF LEADERLY LOVE

What then is the impact of leaderly love? An examination of Lejeune's body of work offers four explanations. First, when love is placed back into leadership, organizations will witness miracles unfold on the battlefield as well as in the boardroom. As Lejeune reflected after surveying major campaigns, "miracles must be wrought if victories are to be won, and to work miracles men's hearts must needs be afire with self-sacrificing love" (Lejeune, 1930, Loc 4146). Tasks that seems impossible to accomplish with fear, become a reality when love is the motive. Second, a refreshing surge of courage will spring forth in the institution when leaderly love becomes the order of the day. Lejeune contends that when commands experience love, "unquenchable courage…to crush out fear" becomes the norm. Likewise, the third impact of leaderly love is a synergistic focus that emerges. Stated in the verbiage of Gabe, an "unconquerable determination" crystalizes in the eyes of the led that says failure is not an option! Fourth, as outlined in the proportional discipline section, love can positively contribute to "a higher state of discipline." Finally, leaderly love can inspire the most hardened warrior to take the hill even if it means to risk limb or to willingly lay down a life for a friend (see Chapter Two for the story of a Sergeant of Marines, a Battalion Commander, and a bridge).

LEADERS EAT LAST

Love from a Marine perspective may best be summarized by the saying, "Leaders eat last." The ensuing story best captures this cultural norm practiced by Lejeune and illustrates the impact it can have on a person as well as an organization.

> He [Lejeune] once reprimanded an officer, in private, for breaking into the chow line in front of enlisted men cued for their meal. "Sir, you will see that your men are fed first and then, and only then, may you feed your face. Do you understand? You need your men. It is they, not you, who will cut the throat out of the Hun." He quietly told the young officer

in private, "You are the scholar, Lieutenant. Your noncommissioned officers are the teachers. Your men are the students. Act like a scholar. You look after your men and they will look after you." Gabe then smiled at the lieutenant and slapped him on the shoulder. Looking him in the eyes, "Let's keep this conversation between us scholars. Okay?" (Bates, 2012, Loc 1507)?

This legendary story is a reminder that eating last is a powerful gesture of leaderly love. When bypassed, the team will be happy to see the likes of such a manager depart. Until they leave, the team will not give their best. In contrast, when this principle is embraced, and leaders make a quality decision to look after the team first, they will indeed discover that such a unit will readily look after that leader. The question now becomes, What are some practical ways to help the 21st-century influencer reinsert love back into their leadership? The following acronym will be used to provide a possible answer— EAT LAST.

Evaluate your heart

Ask for feedback

Trust your people

Lead others the way you want to be led

Arm yourself with coaches

Stay spiritually fit

Temper your ego

EVALUATE YOUR HEART

Perhaps the most difficult element of a leader to evaluate is the heart. It is a very difficult task to discern what truly motives an influencer to be the chief decider. A cursory survey of history will suggest that there is a plethora of reasons why people desire to be in charge. Some of the reasons may include vainglory, a sense of destiny, revenge, or sincere desire to transform an organization. It would be difficult to embrace a philosophy of eating last if one's heart has a natural bent to self-centeredness. To this end, the following survey is designed to help unearth the motives of the heart. Sincerely answer the following questions by circling the response that best describes the leader's behavior.

THE SERVANT-LEADERSHIP ASSESSMENT

1. My first response to organizational dysfunction is to?

    A. Discover who is at fault.

    B. Ask the right question to fix the mess.

2. Which option would others say best describes you?

    A. Hubris.

    B. Humility.

3. Which of the following best describes your view on success?

    A. It is more important to be seen.

    B. It is more important to put in a hard day's work.

4. Which of the following would others say best describes you?

    A. S/he is a politician in every sense of the word.

    B. B. S/he would rather keep her/his good name than play the game.

5. Which option would others say best describes you?

   A. S/he is a champion of organizational "happy talk."

   B. S/he is not afraid to point out the elephant in the room.

6. Which option best describes you?

   A. I am more concerned about being "right."

   B. I am more concerned about the team being "right."

7. Which of the following would others say best describes you?

   A. S/he only treats people with "power" special.

   B. S/he treats everyone the same regardless of their status in life.

THE SERVANT-LEADERSHIP ASSESSMENT SCALE

If you have 7 "Bs" = Congratulations, you are truly the last leader to eat and are making positive change!

If you have 6–5 "Bs" = Your team respects you, and morale is high.

If you have 4–2 "Bs" = Consider attending some training on servant-leadership to help you grow.

If you have 1 "B" = Consider seeking out a servant-leadership coach to help take your game to the next level.

If you have 0 "Bs" = Consider the sentiments of this book and ponder if you are called to lead.

ASK FOR FEEDBACK

For the last few decades, young Americans who desire to become Marine officers are ordered to report to The Basic School (TBS) upon successfully completing the Officer Candidate School (OCS). TBS is essentially the entry level school of leadership where future warriors are exposed to the philosophy of eating last for 26 weeks.

But perhaps one of the most important fibers of this process is the proactive integration of feedback throughout the training. A crucial tool to refine their officership is the giving and receiving of critical advice. This intangible tool is akin to the refining process of converting dull steel into a sharp sword. In like manner, if one were to embrace the servant way, they too must be open to feedback and never be too prideful to ask for it.

TRUST YOUR PEOPLE

Cialdini (2009) makes a compelling case for the law of reciprocation. The theory, which is backed by empirical studies, suggests that people often feel obliged to give back something that was first given to them. To illustrate, if a person were to give someone a birthday card out of the blue, the recipient of such an act will have a higher propensity to return the favor once the giver of the card's birthday came around. If this principle is true, then it would behoove an influencer to genuinely give trust to the team. This small gesture can increase speed and set the conditions for courageous innovation to flourish.

LEAD OTHERS THE WAY YOU WANT TO BE LED

Virtually every person has been on the receiving end of horrible leadership. Typically, the heart of such a manager is filled with hubris, who is in hot pursuit of vainglory, and usually only cares for their own needs. This reality, unfortunately, has left many perplexed and deeply wounded. If, however, anything can be gleaned from such an experience, perhaps the lesson is to lead others the way you want to be led. The golden rule of leadership suggests that other-centered thinking will be more persuasive than narcissism.

ARM YOURSELF WITH COACHES

It has been said that if you want to go fast, go alone. But if you want to go far, go with a team. In today's geo-political realities, gone are the days of Lone Ranger leaders. What are needed now are leaders who will take feedback and operationalize it with their own team of coaches. It should be noted, however, that such coaches should be empowered to speak the truth in love. Otherwise, the hand-selected inner-circle will quickly evolve into a band of puppets that hastens the demise of an organization. Hence, it would behoove an influencer to select coaches that are experienced, courageous, committed to values, and are not moved by fame or fortune.

STAY SPIRITUALLY FIT

Gary Smith, a retired Sergeant Major of Marines best captured the essence of spiritual fitness while serving as a panelist on the same topic at Marine Corps University in 2018. He asserted that, "Whatever is deep down in the well, will come up in the bucket!" One can abstract several principles from this saying. First, one cannot give what one does not have within them. The assumption of leadership is that their well is full and in times of crisis they can safely draw strength from within as well as provide such fortitude to the led. The second assumption that can be made is that the water in the well is healthy or good enough to drink. This supposition may not be the case. Thus, the questions that leaders should ask of themselves to evaluating the heart include, Does the metaphorical water in the well align with the ethos of the organization? Are you running on empty? What is the constant source of your spiritual fitness?

TEMPER YOUR EGO

Contrary to conventional wisdom, it takes more strength of character to temper one's ego than to impulsively lash out in the moment.

Impulsive behaviors are essentially a manifestation of a lack of emotional intelligence (EI). EI is the ability to be emotionally self-aware, able to self-regulate such emotions, show empathy to others, and motivate the led. The motivation aspect as well as trust is undermined when egoism is a constant on display. To this end, learning the art of the tactical pause before engaging, or when possible "sleeping on" the issue, can proactively defuse toxic outbursts.

CONCLUSION

John A. Lejeune's collective work suggests that he was a fierce proponent of leaderly love. He also understood that this missing ingredient of influence was vital to unlock the dormant potential of organizations as well as the people that dare to support them. Somewhere along the way, unfortunately, a model of influencing has emerged that treats people as objects, numbers, or merely hired hands and not as hired hearts (Winston, 2002). Perhaps this pathway is easier in the short term because one does not have to deal with the challenging work of loving. John A. Lejeune knew that exercising leaderly love is not for the faint of heart, but only for the few. For it is the few and the proud who unapologetically teach that under no circumstance will you leave a Marine behind. Whether on a battlefield or when someone is alone and struggling with an issue, the rhetoric of the Corps agrees with the sentiments of this chapter. Stated slightly differently, the saying goes that a happy wife makes a happy life. When leaders dare to EAT LAST, they too will embrace what Lejeune always knew—happy Marines will keep our honor clean. After all, "a happy and contented detachment is usually a well-disciplined detachment" (Lejeune, 1930, Loc 6281).

CHAPTER SEVEN

FROM COMMAND & CONTROL TO COMMAND & FEEDBACK

"The Command and Control of the future is Command and Feedback."

-James Mattis

The fifth question that a researcher needs to explore to understand whether or not a person is a servant-leader is, Are the served more autonomous? To explore if this trait existed in a Lejeunian style of influence, it would be prudent to first define the term *autonomous*. Iarocci (2018) frames the autonomy factor by asking, Do those served have more control over their own decisions and lives? Are they empowered? Good servant-leadership involves the sharing of power, not the hoarding of it. This notion of sharing authority and empowering the led is the bedrock of servant-leadership. Unfortunately, the sources that directly speak to this point are limited. However, there seems to be enough circumstantial evidence to safely infer that Lejeune was indeed a champion of empowerment.

> It will be necessary for officers not only to devote their close attention to the many questions affecting the comfort, health, morals, religious guidance, military training, and discipline of the men under their command, but also to actively enlist the interest of their men in building up and maintaining their bodies in the finest physical condition; to encourage them to improve their professional knowledge and to make every effort by means of historical, educational, and patriotic addresses to cultivate in the hearts a deep abiding love of the Corps and Country. (Lejeune, 1930)

The first anecdotal evidence that points toward an autonomous ideology is found above. In this message to the officer community, Lejeune was setting the conditions for empowerment. Particularly, the encouragement of the leader to improve the led "by means of historical, educational, and patriotic addresses to cultivate in the hearts a deep abiding love of the Corps and Country" is paramount. The premise of such an exhortation was designed to shape followership to embrace what Krulak (1999) would later frame as *The Strategic Corporal*. The following best summarizes the sentiments of this term

> Regrettably, the end of the Cold War heralded not the hoped for era of peace, but rather, a troubling age characterized by global disorder, pervasive crisis, and the constant threat of chaos. Since 1990, the Marine Corps has responded to crises at a rate equal to three times that of the Cold War—on average, once every five weeks. On any given day, up to 29,000 Marines are forward deployed around the world. In far-flung places like Kenya, Indonesia, and Albania, they have stood face-to-face with the perplexing and hostile challenges of the chaotic post–Cold War world for which the "rules" have not yet been written. The three-block war was not simply a fanciful metaphor for future conflicts—it is reality. Like Corporal Hernandez, today's Marines have already encountered its great challenges and they have been asked to exercise an exceptional degree of maturity, restraint, and judgment.... They behaved as Marines always have and as we expect today's Marines and those of the future to behave—with courage, with aggressiveness, and with resolve. The future battlefields on which Marines fight will be increasingly hostile, lethal, and chaotic. Our success will hinge, as it always has, on the leadership of our junior Marines. We must ensure that they are prepared to lead. (Krulak, 1999)

The strategic corporal concept adheres to the commander's intent (assuming such direction is legal, moral, and prudent) and invokes courage, aggressiveness, judgment, maturity, restraint, as well as resolve to achieve the mission. This construct would not unfold in the context of a micro-managerial environment where some leaders bottleneck decisions that should be made at the lowest level. When, however, the principles of empowerment are intentionally cultivated, the likes of one of Lejeune's most commendable enlisted Marines emerge—John Quick. Gabe observed the following about this giant of a Marine.

> Perhaps of all the Marines I ever knew, Quick approached more nearly the perfect type of noncommissioned officer. A calm, forceful, intelligent, loyal and courageous man he was. I never knew him to raise his voice, lose his temper, or use profane language, and yet he exacted and obtained prompt and explicit obedience from all persons subject to his orders. (Lejeune, 1930, Loc 1254)

This second piece of evidence that Lejeune was indeed an advocate of the autonomous factor rests in the above sentiments given about Quick. Such a tribute opens the door to explore questions such as, Who exactly was John Quick, what was his legacy, and why was Lejeune such an enthusiastic admirer?

JOHN QUICK: THE MAN

According to the history division of the Marine Corps, John H. Quick was born on 20 June 1870 in Charleston, West Virginia. At the age of 22 this legendary influencer enlisted in the Marines Corps in Philadelphia, Pennsylvania, on 10 August 1982. Due to poor health, unfortunately, he would be forced to retire on 15 September 1920 at the age of 50. But before exploring further the career path that made Quick a household name, the reader's attention will be momentarily placed upon the traits that arrested Lejeune's attention and propelled Quick to become that "nearly perfect type of noncommissioned officer" in Lejeune's mind. Such traits, to emphasize the point, are also what embody an autonomous follower.

THE CALM FACTOR

The first mannerism that Lejeune commended about Quick was his calm demeanor. It was as if the 13th Commandant knew that this trait was imperative for warfighting. From a practical point of view, the friction and fog of war creates a chaotic environment. What one does not need is more uncertainty in such a context. On the contrary, a personality with the natural propensity to be cool under pressure, regardless of the issue, can indeed be a game changer. It can be a difference maker largely because this mannerism can effortlessly calm others as well as reach clear-headed decisions. The empirical research seems to align success with this trait in leaders. Specifically, Russell (20016) discovered that 90% of top performers were able to manage their emotions in times of stress to stay calm and in control. Thus, the calming factor of Quick as well as others is what distinguished him from the rest.

THE CHARISMA FACTOR

The second feature that Lejeune used to describe Quick's temperament was forcefulness. One can argue that this dynamic is closely related to charisma or the "it" factor. Yulk (2010, p. 309) suggests that this term is used to describe a form of influence based not on tradition or formal authority but rather on follower perceptions that the leader is endowed with exceptional qualities. The "it" factor transcends position and commands a level of respect that others would be willing to bend their will to. In the case of Quick, the evidence suggests that he never used such gifts for selfish ambition. On the contrary, this autonomous follower used his forcefulness for the benefit of the team. This by-product of servant-leadership helps to unearth such attributes in the led and sets the condition for them to activate the "it" factor even under the most stressful scenarios.

THE CLEVER FACTOR

Perhaps one of the most overlooked elements of an autonomous follower is the ability to be critical in thought. According to Kelly (1988), such followers know how to think for themselves and carry out their duties and assignments with energy and assertiveness. This very description is exactly what Lejeune observed in John Quick. More specifically, Lejeune applauded Quick's intelligence as a non-commissioned officer. This ability to think critically about people, processes, and policies is a tremendous benefit to organizations. Servant-leaders, like Lejeune, understand this reality and proactively equip followers with the tools to sharpen their minds as well as to strengthen their bodies.

THE COMMITMENT FACTOR

Autonomous followers like John Quick are incredibly loyal. This fourth attribute that Lejeune saluted in Quick is not to be confused with blind loyalty. Blind commitment is dedicated to a person with no questions asked. This form of allegiance breeds organizational toxicity and undermines the principles of the oath of office that people like Quick took. The form of loyalty that autonomous followers employ is to principles and not personalities, the office and not officers. To this end, the likes of John Quick and others solemnly affirm to support and defend the Constitution of the United States against all enemies, foreign and domestic; to bear true faith and allegiance to the same; and to obey the orders of the President of the United States and the orders of the officers appointed over me, according to regulations and the Uniform Code of Military Justice. To this end, the commitment factor of an autonomous follower is what separates great organizations from good ones.

THE COURAGEOUS FACTOR

Perhaps the calling card of an autonomous follower is their courage. Buford (2018) argued that there are four forms of courage: battle-field, boardroom, by-stander, and basic. Basic courage is a person's ability to discern that they are in pain and, instead of suffering quietly, they muster up the fortitude to get specialized help. By-stander courage recognizes that something is wrong amongst peers. Because of this, an influencer engages in a prudent manner. Boardroom courage is a follower's ability to speak truth to power for the sake of organizational health. The final form of valor is what John Quick exemplified—battlefield courage. The following citations best captures his intrepidness.

MEDAL OF HONOR

The President of the United States of America, in the name of Congress, takes pleasure in presenting the Medal of Honor to Sergeant John Henry Quick (MCSN: 68644), United States Marine Corps, for extraordinary heroism while serving with the 1st Marine (Huntington's) Battalion, in action during the battle of Cuzco, Cuba, 14 June 1898. Sergeant Quick distinguishing himself during this action. Quick signaled the U.S.S. Dolphin on three different occasions while exposed to a heavy fire from the enemy (Medal of Honor Citation awarded 7 July 1899 for actions during the Spanish-American War).

DISTINGUISHED SERVICE CROSS

The President of the United States of America, authorized by Act of Congress, July 9, 1918, takes pleasure in presenting the Distinguished Service Cross to Sergeant Major John Henry Quick (MCSN: 68644), United States Marine Corps, for extraordinary heroism while serving with the Headquarters Company, Sixth Regiment (Marines), 2d Division, A.E.F., in action at Bouresches, France, 6 June 1918. Sergeant Major Quick volunteered and assisted in taking a truck load of ammunition and material into Bouresches, France, over a road swept by artillery and machine-gun fire, thereby relieving a critical situation (Distinguished Service Cross awarded for actions during WWI).

NAVY CROSS

The President of the United States of America takes pleasure in presenting the Navy Cross to Sergeant Major John Henry Quick (MCSN: 68644), United States Marine Corps, for extraordinary heroism while serving with the Headquarters Company, 6th Regiment (Marines), 2d Division, A.E.F. in action at Bouresches, France, 6 June 1918. Sergeant Major Quick volunteered and assisted in taking a truck load of ammunition and material into Bouresches, France, over a road swept by artillery and machine-gun fire, thereby relieving a critical situation (Navy Cross awarded for actions during WWI).

Though there are no public records of the other forms of courage (i.e., boardroom, by-stander, and basic), no one can question Quick's mettle on the battlefield. As indicated above, this aspect of an autonomous follower was essential then and is also a necessity for the 21st-century warrior or worker. The question at this point that goes beyond the scope of this section becomes, How well do entities develop courage in organizational citizens, and what does right look like regarding courage development?

THE CLEAN FACTOR

One can argue that John Quick took to heart the third line of the Marine Corps Hymn. As a reminder, it resounds that Marines are "first to fight for right and freedom and to keep our honor clean." Without question Quick was not afraid to fight and, according to Lejeune, he also was a champion of keeping honor clean. How? Quick seemingly knew that in order to impact a larger culture, one must master the little things well. In the case of this Sergeant Major of Marines, he set the example by living a clean life and never used profane language. This may seem farfetched that a Marine would subscribe to this feature but, it is what made him such an admired personality. This fact begs the question, Does the usage of profanity bring value to leadership or does it undermine it?

THE CREDIBILITY FACTOR

There is an old proverb that says, "He that thinketh he leadth, and hath no one following, is only taking a walk." Such a proverb would not apply to the likes of John Quick simply because of the respect he demanded from others. This autonomous follower had what is known as "street cred." This ability in the sentiments of Lejeune to exact and obtain prompt and enthusiastic obedience from all persons subject to his orders was the sum total of the various factors outlined above. In a sense, Quick earned respect by the virtue of his being, not by the rank on his collar. The credibility factor of Quick only increased as he served in every campaign during his era and within various commands in the Corps.

THE AUTONOMOUS FOLLOWERSHIP OF LEJEUNE

One can argue that leaders often gravitate to followers that resemble themselves. Such an assertion, admittedly, can have both a positive and negative connotation. The undesirable aspect of this premise will be explored more in Chapter Eleven. For now, the question that demands an answer is, What were the moments in Lejeune's life that created an appreciation for autonomous followership as exhibited by John Quick? An examination of Lejeune's collective body of work points to three distinct data points.

THE VIGILANCE COMMITTEE MODEL

Some decades after the assassination of President Abraham Lincoln in 1865, young John Lejeune received a life-altering lesson. From the point of view of the Lejeune family, the local government of Louisiana where they lived was not working efficiently and was corrupt. Disunity was on the rise, insurrections were the order of the day, and their private property was being threatened. It was in this context that Lejeune wrote

We lost fourteen head of cattle in the Spring of one year in this way. It is not surprising, therefore, the decent white men should have organized themselves for self-protection and to secure the blessings and peace and tranquility for their families. In Pointe Coupee Parish the organization did not take the form of a Ku Klux Klan, as was the case in many of the Southern states. Instead, in our community a local Vigilance Committee was organized which, although it did not form a part of a larger organization, nevertheless worked in harmony with other similar committees in near-by communities and parishes. My father was the captain of the Vigilance Committee and was ably assisted by several young lieutenants, among them Dr. William B. Archer, son of my uncle and aunt, Dr. and Mrs. John Archer. (Lejeune, 1930, Loc 233)

The possible lesson that young Lejeune learned from one of the most influential men in his life was the art and science of being an autonomous follower. He watched his father exercise calm, clever, charismatic, and courageous influence when they perceived their leaders were no longer relevant. This notion of standing up or creating vigilance committees in the face of wrong would become the subconscious model that Gabe would employ throughout his life.

THE NAVAL ACADEMY'S RECOMMENDATION

The second data point where one can see Lejeune's autonomous followership on display was at the Academy. At the completion of his time at Annapolis, he was informed that he did not receive his desired choice. Instead, the academic board recommended Lejeune to the Engineer Corps. Consider his sentiments in the following lengthy quote

I was bitterly disappointed and intensely indignant, my indignation being stronger even than my disappointment, because I felt very keenly the sting of injustice. I had worked hard for six years and had succeeded in obtaining a class standing sufficiently high to warrant the belief that I was entitled to be assigned to the corps or branch which I had requested. My indignation was further stimulated by the fact that while my wishes had been completely ignored, the wishes of juniors in class standing had, in nearly all instances, been granted. I therefore immediately came to the determination to do everything honorable in my power to overturn the decision of the Academic Board in my case. Hayward and I spent the evening discussing the subject and mapping out a plan of campaign. I decided that, first of all, I would endeavor to induce the members of the Academic Board to change their decision, and early the next morning I called on my good friends, Lieutenant and Mrs. E. K. Moore, to obtain the benefit of their advice. They advised me to see Commander Asa Walker and Chief Engineer Milligan, two members of the Board, which I promptly did, and learned that Heyward's information was correct. I exhausted every argument I could think of in the endeavor to secure their support of a proposal to have the Board reconsider its action at a meeting to be held that day. I also told them that if the assignment were not changed, the action of the board would be tantamount to forcing me out of the service, as I would resign as soon as I could find other employment in civil life. (Lejeune, 1930, Loc 1161)

Though the first phase of his plan to overrule the board's decision didn't work, he persisted nonetheless until justice was served. As highlighted above, Lejeune viewed the board's decision as wrong largely because others junior to him received their request and he didn't despite his hard-academic work. Thus, Lejeune took his appeal directly to the Superintendent, Captain W. T. Sampson.

Upon patiently listening to Lejeune, the superintendent upheld the board's decision and offered the following reason. "First, they deemed it important to assign graduates of ability to the Engineer Corps; second, I was the only member of the upper block who had not applied for the Line as first choice; and third, because the Board considered that I stood too high in the class to be assigned to the Marine Corps" (Lejeune, 1930, Loc 1172). Though this bold move was unsuccessful, that didn't stop Gabe's campaign. On the contrary, he reached out to his senator and a meeting was arranged with the Secretary of the Navy Department. At the meeting Lejeune successfully outlined his case and persuaded the secretary to call the superintendent. While in the meeting the secretary called Captain Sampson and said, "Commodore, I want this young man assigned to the Marine Corps." Thus, Lejeune's own version of a vigilance committee proved successful as he invoked the principles of an autonomous follower.

THE SLEEPING GENERAL

The final data point that illustrates Lejeune's autonomous followership involves the case of the sleeping general. As the commanding general of the Second Division during WWI, he was directed "to march south to Dun-sur-Meuse, and on the following day cross the river and march to Stenay, preliminary to jumping off from that place on 17 November." Lejeune knew that this wasn't a prudent order because his men were exhausted from fighting, and he knew that a more convenient crossing point made more sense. To this end, Lejeune pushed back and insisted that such an order be modified. The duty officer that conveyed the order to Lejeune indicated that he didn't have the authority to oblige such a request. Lejeune then explains:

> I then asked that the matter be taken up with the appropriate officer with the view of obtaining a modification of the orders. He said that all the higher officers were asleep and he did not care to wake them. I replied, "It is better to wake up one General than to have twenty-five thousand sick and exhausted men march sixty kilometers, and I will do so myself." He then said he would deliver my message. In a few minutes he called back, saying that he was directed to inform me that the bridge at Stenay would be repaired, that the march to Dun-sur-Meuse would not take place, and that the march to Stenay could be made on the afternoon of 16 November. I have given the details of this conversation not with any intent to criticize a loyal and faithful officer, but in order to illustrate the importance of sometimes being rather determined and persistent when necessary to protect the welfare of the officers and men under one's command. (Lejeune, 1930, Loc 5629)

One can abstract from the above rendition several key points that further prove Lejeune's autonomous followership tendencies. First, one can see the sincere concern for the led. The men were exhausted, and if such an order were fulfilled, many would have become ill or possibly died. Lejeune was not afraid of the risks of war, but he was opposed to unnecessary hazards. Second, one can see determination and persistence manifested in his actions with no regard to himself. Finally, this disregard for self could easily be interpreted as a form of boardroom courage that is vital for followership.

THE MAKING OF AN AUTONOMOUS FOLLOWER

The vigilance committee lesson abstracted from his father, the Naval academy example, and the case of the sleeping general are possible reasons why Lejeune celebrated SgtMaj John Quick. But how specifically do servant-leaders create the conditions for followers to be more autonomous? To explore and provide a possible answer to this question, the ensuing acronym will be invoked—EMPOWER.

Educate

Motivate

Proclaim historical examples

Operationalize crucibles

Why-proof your decisions

Eradicate a zero-defect culture

Resiliency training for the 21ˢᵗ century

Educate

The first step towards building an environment conducive to autonomous followership is education. It is interesting to note that the term *education* is derived from the Latin word *educare*, which means to "bring up, lead forth, or to extract out." In the sentiments of Lejeune, this aspect of leadership should in no wise be overlooked. On the contrary, servants can bring up, lead forth, and extract out autonomous behaviors by invoking the principles outlined in Chapter Five. By employing such principles, unhealthy paradigms are challenged and one's perspective can be recalibrated to embrace a more excellent way.

MOTIVATE

Daniel H. Pink in his book *Drive* outlines three key principles to activate intrinsic motivation. Ironically, the first key points toward an ideology that people desire to direct their own life and not have it dictated to them. When followers clearly understand that leadership desires this for them and creates the space for this construct to unfold, productivity increases. Second, Pink argues that followers have a deep desire to move toward mastery. Mastery implies that leadership intentionally creates opportunities for followers to improve. Finally, Pink rounds out his argument by suggesting that people need a purpose. Such a purpose, when found, can not only inspire organizational citizens to new heights, but it can also combat self-destructive behaviors that often undermine operations.

PROCLAIM HISTORICAL EXAMPLES

In the context of organizations, a plethora of traditions help define its mission. Some of those customs are indeed beneficial, but others may inadvertently weaken core values. To this end, it is critical for leaders to take the best of organizational traditions and highlight followers that dared to be autonomous such as SgtMaj John Quick for the Marine Corps. This usage of historical means can help to cultivate an appreciation of an entity's past as well as make a case that the practice of this form of followership is applicable for now and the future.

OPERATIONALIZE CRUCIBLES

General Charles C. Krulak makes the case that one of the key mechanisms to develop the strategic corporal is unchanged. He states, "bold, capable, and intelligent men and women of character are drawn to the Corps, and are recast in the crucible of recruit training, where time honored methods instill deep within them the Corps' enduring ethos." This notion of being recast in the crucible should not be considered a single event in time but an intentional and strategic continuum throughout the career of a follower. In other words, it would serve commands well to replicate moments that challenge followers with crucible-like experiences to be more autonomous while they adhere to their commander's intent.

WHY-PROOF YOUR DECISIONS

The premise of Simon Sinek's popular book *Start with Why* can be referenced to explain the fifth point of the empower model. To galvanize followers toward autonomous behaviors, leaders should endeavor to why-proof their decisions. As Sinek illustrates, there is a tendency for influencers to start with the what (i.e., take the hill) or the how (i.e., take the hill on their flank) and not with the why (i.e., we need this hill to win the battle and to provide us with a tactical advantage). When leaders why-proof their decisions, they effortlessly cultivate the purpose of both the follower and gain buy-in into the directive. This practical yet profound point not only creates synergy, it can increase organizational speed.

ERADICATE A ZERO-DEFECT CULTURE

Perhaps the quickest way to suffocate innovation, undermine calculated risk taking, and inadvertently encourage passive behaviors is to establish a zero-defect culture. Moreover, such a culture can possibly suppress the growth of the next generation of leaders if one is not careful. To illustrate this point, consider the following fitness report:

> Good in professional ability and general conduct . . . Excellent in sobriety and health [but] not good in attention to duty and efficiency of the men under his command. The [Marines] under this officer are not trustworthy as sentries and are not tidy and soldierly in appearance. The officer is apparently too indolent and lacking in zeal; he does not give the personal attention to his men that he should; the result is a want of efficiency in the guard.

After observing this officer continue to display the above behaviors, if you oversaw this follower, what would you do? Would you tolerate (do nothing), treat (address the manner immediately), or terminate (relieve this leader for cause)? A respectable number of the people that I have had the honor of posing this question to have chosen terminate. Let's continue to unfold the rest of this case study by showing how the person in charge responded to the above fitness report.

> [These reports have] greatly disappointed me both as regards to you and the fact that the Corps has been so poorly represented on board the Bennington, and your record as an officer will be greatly affected unless you pay closer attention to your duties.

The above counsel from Major General Charles Heywood to a young officer named John A. Lejeune was enough treatment to spur this Marine to step up his game. If, however, Major General Heywood had employed a zero-defect decision and terminated

Lejeune, the Corps could have very well been without one of its most prolific thinkers and leaders of all time.

RESILIENCY TRAINING FOR THE 21ST CENTURY

The final component of the empower model is resiliency training. Again, Krulak asserts that an institutional commitment to lifelong professional development should be the order of the day. In the context of 21st-century warfare and considering the growing self-destructive tendencies of some service members, it would be a logical step to train to the standard of resiliency. It is not enough to assume that those who volunteer to serve in the armed forces have the wherewithal to function in the fog of war or, more importantly, to live with themselves after the fog has subsided. To this end, training that leads followers to explore how specifically they will bounce back from life's traumas in a way that helps them grow, should be considered.

CONCLUSION

Though the evidence was not overwhelming, there are sufficient historical examples that Lejeune created, modeled, and advocated for the building of an autonomous follower. Not only was this construct important to the 13th Commandant, it is an imperative for the Honorable James Mattis. As he reflected on the challenges of tomorrow's fight, Mattis argued that the command and control of the future will be command and feedback. If this is true, and in order for this system to properly maneuver at an optimum level, autonomous followers must be built. The proven method to develop this form of followership is the practice of servant-leadership as demonstrated by the likes of John A. Lejeune.

Kneecap to Kneecap Discussion

1. On a scale of 1 to 5 (5 being the highest), rate how well you believe your organization develops followers to be autonomous? Please discuss why you graded your organization as you did, and explain what contributes to such a grade.

2. Lejeune commended John Quick as an exemplar of a noncommissioned officer. In his commendation, he highlighted some of his attributes, which for this book are referred to as the traits of an autonomous follower (Calm, Charisma, Clever, Committed, Courageous, Clean, and Credibility). Discuss which are the most important for a follower to have and why.

3. Three examples were provided to highlight Lejeune's propensity to be an autonomous follower: the vigilance committee model, the Naval Academy model, and the waking the sleeping general model. Have a conversation about which one of the examples resonated the most with you and why.

4. Reread the principles affiliated with the EMPOWER acronym. Have a conversation on which element(s) of the acronym can help to develop followers in your organization now.

5. This chapter began and concluded with a statement from the Honorable James Mattis. Take a position for or against the assertion (i.e., the command and control of the future will be command and feedback) and defend your case.

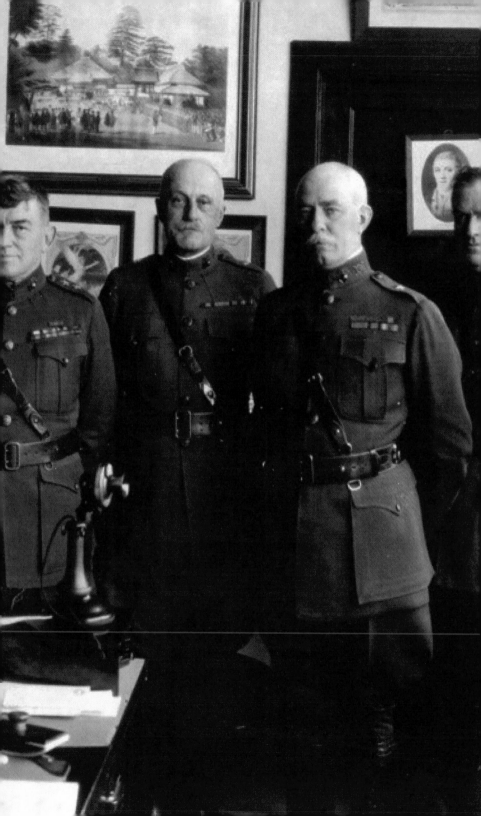

CHAPTER EIGHT

FOLLOW ME, AS I SERVE!

"Leadership is the sum total of those qualities of intellect, human understanding, and moral character that enables a person to inspire and control a group of people successfully."

-John A. Lejeune

The sixth question that a researcher needs to explore to understand whether or not a person is a servant is, Will those served have the propensity to serve others when they are in charge? Stated slightly differently, will the recipients of servant-leadership become transformed enough to inspire others in a similar fashion? In an endeavor to investigate this question, the focus of this chapter will be placed on a personality that was on the receiving end of a Lejeunian style of influencing the longest. Considering the previous chapter, it seems only fitting to begin the conversation with the following quote.

> John Quick was a Sergeant in my Company, said General Neville. A force of Marines was dispatched to dislodge the Spaniards at Cuzco a few miles from Guantanamo on the coast. My company, including Sergeant Quick, went along. A wild little fight resulted, during which it became necessary to signal to the gunboat Dolphin to shell the Spaniards. It was a blazing bitter hot day on top of the ridge with its shrived chaparral and its straight tall cactus plants. The sky was bare and blue and hurt like brass. The Marines were red and sweating like so many hull-buried stokers in the tropics. A signal-man was called for to communicate with the Dolphin. John Quick was laying on his stomach near me pumping his Lee rifle at the Spaniards. He said, "I can do it." I told him to try. He tied a large blue flag which he obtained from the Cubans to a long-crooked stick and started wig-wagging. He tried for 20 minutes to get the signal to the Dolphin, but that ship was unable to read his message against the background. So Quick had to place himself on the top of the ridge and outline himself and his flag against the sky. As soon as the

concealed Spaniards caught sight of the silhouette they let go like mad at him. To make things more comfortable for Quick the situation demanded that he face the sea and turn his back to the Spanish bullets. A hard game, mark you—to stand with the small of your back to that leaden hail. We gazed at him, marveling every second that he had not yet pitched headlong. As I looked at John Quick wig-wagging there against the sky, I would not have given a tin tobacco-tag for his life. Escape for him seemed hopeless, yet Quick signaled on as if he were on the parade ground instead of standing exposed to those Spanish bullets that drifted by him or spurted up the dust near his feet. Each bullet sought his life, but John Quick's message reached the Dolphin and when he dropped down beside me, I felt as if he had returned from the grave. He was awarded the Medal of Honor for that wonderful act of courage. (Anonymous, 1931)

The above version of Wendell Cushing Neville's leader-member exchange with Quick as well as his rendition of a remarkable account of valor warrants a discussion. The first question this story generates is, Is it possible that Neville's style of leadership was a contributing factor to Quick's courageous actions that was displayed 14 June 1898? As we outlined in Chapter Seven, autonomous followers display key traits that are often brought out with servant-leadership. This assertion is not by any means meant to detract from the bravery that John Quick showed that day. On the contrary, the record is clear that his mettle rose to the occasion time after time. What the reader should consider, however, is that the servant-leadership style that Neville modeled was a possible antecedent to the moment.

Contemplate the following principles that one can abstract from the above story. First, note the fact that Quick was a recipient of Neville's leadership long before this fight. What is not known with absolute certainty is how long Quick was in Neville's company and the intentional lessons he taught to his men. But one can glean insights from this account as well as from other sources to safely make a conclusion. To illustrate, notice the location of the leader and the led during this engagement, "John Quick was laying on his stomach near me pumping his Lee rifle at the Spaniards." Seemingly, Neville knew that his place was not on the ship, nor in the back, but in harm's way with his command. Perhaps it was this form of leaderly love that inspired Quick to say without hesitation to his company commander, "I can do it." Perhaps it was the fact that his leader as well as brothers in arms inspired him to risk his life by willingly exposing himself to danger. Neville described it right when he said, "when he dropped down beside me, I felt as if he had returned from the grave." Quick went to the gates of hell, this author would argue, largely because that's what followers do when their leaders have a history of eating last and empowering the led with simple words like, "try."

SERVING TOGETHER

Let's now consider the question, Who is Wendell Cushing Neville? According to the Naval Academy's wall of notable graduates, "Wendell C. Neville was born at Portsmouth, Virginia, on 12 May 1870. He graduated from the Naval Academy in the class of 1890 and was commissioned a second lieutenant in the Marine Corps in 1892. He was brevetted to captain in 1898 for his outstanding leadership and valor at Guantanamo Bay, and in 1900 he was commended for gallantry for his role in the China Relief Expedition. In 1914, Neville led the Marines ashore at Veracruz, Mexico, and was awarded the Medal of Honor for conspicuous gallantry. During World War I, he commanded the 5th Marines at Belleau Wood and later rose to command of the 4th Marine Brigade."

An analysis of the career paths of Lejeune and Neville reveal that there were several occasions when they served together. The first overlapping point was at the Naval Academy. Though Lejeune graduated in 1888 and Neville hailed from the class of 1890, there is no record of them formally interacting with one another. However, one can safely infer that both were adequately prepared to enter the service with a keen sense of patriotism and selflessness because "the system of education was thorough and was conducted in a most conscientious and able manner by the instructors. The discipline was severe, but salutary" (Lejeune, 1930, Loc 553).

The second time the two influencers served together was with the 2nd Advance Base Regiment. During this time, the newly selected Colonel Lejeune oversaw Lt Col Neville. It was from this platform that Lejeune became impressed with Neville's abilities. Venzon and Gordon (2008) illuminates this point by stating that, "John A. Lejeune, made a point of Neville's efficiency and zealous approach to duty and attributed the success of the regiment in the field to Neville's performance. Lejeune felt strongly that he deserved special mention" (p. 92). Soon after such accolades were given, the Regiment was directed to depart for Veracruz, Mexico, to engage in the occupation of the city. While on the grounds, Neville displayed the essence of his leadership and earned the medal of honor. The following citation speaks for itself.

For distinguished conduct in battle engagements of Vera Cruz 21 and April 22, 1914. In command of the Second Regiment

Marines, Lieutenant Colonel Neville was in both days' fighting and almost continually under fire from soon after landing, about noon on the 21st, until we were in possession of the city, about noon of the 22nd. His duties required him to be at points of great danger in directing his officers and men, and exhibited conspicuous courage, coolness and skill in his conduct of the fighting. Upon his courage and skill depended, in great measure, success or failure. His responsibilities were great, and he met them in a manner worthy of commendation. G.O. Navy Department, No. 177, 4 DEC 1915.

Much like the first engagement at Cuzco a few miles from Guantanamo with John Quick, one does not see Neville in the back but right amid the fight, serving. Without question, his men did not want to let Neville down. His coolness was an inspiration and perhaps functioned as a source of calm that motivated the men in the fog of this fight. In the end, it was his courageous skill in his conduct that carried the day. In addition to the above medal of honor, Lejeune's remarks were "glowing as to his eminent fitness for command and recommended him for instruction at the Army War College" (Venzon and Gordon, 2008, p. 95). Are there other clues to help the reader better understand the essence of Neville's conduct?

To peruse this question, the reader's attention is placed on the 5 December 1917 decision for Colonel Neville to assume command of the 5th Regiment in France that would ultimately engage in one of the most iconic battles of the Corps. Though the 5th Regiment was in reserves, they were directed to form a brick wall to protect the French capital from the offensive attack of the Germans. Venzon and Gordon (2008, p. 98) explains that

The first five days of June 1918, the Germans made assault after assault against the marines, only to be repulsed by a thin line of riflemen and machine guns. While they held their position, demoralized remnants of the French units who had met the initial German attack withdrew in a ragged stream through the American lines. One French colonel retreating with his troops pleaded with Neville to join in the withdrawal. Shocked by the suggestion, Neville ignored the advice and held his ground. The French trudged on. Eventually Germans faced Americans along a line from Les Mares Farm to Monneaux.

Upon holding the line, Neville's 5th Regiment was directed to go on the offensive at a place called Belleau Wood. It was primarily the leadership and service of Neville to his men and his country that enabled the Marines to do the impossible—take a stronghold and turn the course of history. Lejeune reflects on this moment when he visited Neville by saying:

> It was a thrilling afternoon we spent at the Fifth Marin Headquarters listening to the stories of the heroic exploits of the officers and men who had stormed machine-gun nests, bayonetted the defenders, made raids by night and by day, and had gained a moral ascendancy over the enemy which they maintained until complete victory crowned their efforts, in spite of hunger, thirst, fatigue, sleeplessness, danger, wounds, and death. It is indeed fitting that Belleau Woods should have been converted into a memorial to the great souled men who fought, suffered and died there. Let us trust that the loving hearts of patriotic Americans will maintain it forever. (Lejeune, 1930, Loc 3545)

For the leadership displayed in battle, both Lejeune and Neville received authorization from President Wilson to be promoted to Major General and Brigadier General, respectively. Moreover, they were both given more responsibility as the Commanding General of the Division and the Commander of 4th Brigade (Marine). At the end of the war, Lejeune, Neville, and the forces were received with a parade in Washington, D.C. Soon afterward, Lejeune was handed the commandancy and Neville was chosen to be the assistant commandant. From this position, Neville for three years had the unique opportunity to observe up close and learn the Lejeunian way of serving. Though Neville was later assigned to become the Commanding General of the Department of the Pacific, he still embraced the servant way as he led the corps through various exercises that the Nation would glean lessons from for future battles. In 1927 he was ordered back to Quantico, Virginia. It was from this command that Lejeune stepped down as the commandant. But as his last official act of duty, Lejeune

> Strongly recommended Major General Neville as my successor. He had **served** [emphasis mine] with me in the Second Division as the Commanding General of the 4th Brigade and on several other occasions, and it was my belief that his record was such to make his appointment desirable. President Coolidge and Secretary Wilbur approved my recommendation, and he was at once nominated and confirmed by the Senate to take office on March 4th, after the inauguration of President Hoover. (Lejeune, 1930, Loc 6569)

SERVANT-LEADERSHIP: IS IT TAUGHT OR CAUGHT?

The reader is invited to observe closely the verbiage from the above recommendation from Lejeune. The inference implies that the current commandant had a large vote in who should be the one to take the Corps to the next level. Notice first the verb that Lejeune chose to use—served. The dictionary states that to serve means to be of use, help, assist, aid, contribute to or to do something for in obedience. What is interesting is Lejeune's subtle use of the term when he says, "He [Neville] served with me...." Not that Neville worked for him or that he commanded this General. This wordsmith intentionally used this wording because this is the essence of servant-leadership. Moreover, because servant-leaders seek to create more servants and not followers (Iarocci, 2018), it can be argued that Lejeune knew that Neville was ready and offered that critical verb—serve—as proof.

But what really garnered Lejeune's confidence in Neville's ability to be the next top Marine in the Corp? Indeed, Neville's record was clear and spoke for itself. What his record did not capture, however, were the intangibles as well as the question, Is servant-leadership taught or caught? To provide a plausible answer to this inquiry, Albert Bandura's social learning theory is invoked into the discourse. Bandura (1977) suggests that, "Leaning would be exceedingly laborious, not to mention hazardous, if people had to rely solely on the effects of their own action to inform them what to do. Fortunately, most human behavior is learned observationally through modeling: from observing others one forms an idea of how new behaviors are performed, and on later occasions this coded information serves as a guide for action" (p. 22).

From the rank of Lieutenant Colonel to Major General, Neville had the unique honor of observing John A. Lejeune's model of the servant way in the worst and best of times. Lejeune knew Neville had excellent opportunities to observe the servant-leadership way via social learning. Likewise, Lejeune was able to observe Neville's servant style as well. This enactment of social learning may have been a contributing factor to Lejeune's recommendation. Servant-leadership is more caught (modeled) than taught (instructional). Though instruction provides the baseline for one to transform, Bandura would submit that the led must be first presented with a model of what right looks like and then right can be caught. In keeping with previous chapters, the following acronym is offered to help influencers positively shape their organizations—CAUGHT.

Create a culture of servant-leaders

Accept the resignation of hubris leaders

Unlearn toxic behaviors

Galvanize servant-leadership training

Habitually communicate servant messages

Toast servant behaviors

CREATE A CULTURE OF SERVANT-LEADERS
One of the key responsibilities of a leader is to make critical decisions. Such decisions are often manifested in policy as well as the filling of key positions. As in the case of Lejeune recommending Neville to become the 14th Commandant of the Marine Corps, so do leaders have an opportunity to shape the future of their respective entities. To this end, it is imperative, in the sentiments of Collins (2001), to put the right people on the bus and in the right seats. For the sake of this chapter, such personalities are those with a proven

track record of competence, character, and who capture the servant way. The empirical evidence suggests that when such a person is at the helm, they outperform others that ascribe to a different brand of influencing (Collins, 2001). To this end, it will take courage to go against the grain and not endorse the popular one for the position but to recommend that servant whose heart is sincerely dedicated to the efficiency of the team without fanfare.

ACCEPT THE RESIGNATION OF HUBRIS LEADERS

The ugly reality is that most hubris leaders are legitimately gifted. This grace has, unfortunately, convinced them that they are the smartest or talented person in the room. This mind-set is the very thing that keeps them from being an active listener and inadvertently creates unnecessary drama and confusion. Moreover, the talent of the hubris leader meets the bottom line at the expense of the people who make the line a reality. This way of business in the interim may be acceptable, but it will destroy the institution in the long run. As such, new regimes should accept the resignation of leaders who believe it is all about them at the soonest if the behavior is not immediately corrected. Otherwise, this influencer will quickly become what Lejeune describes as a coward and a skulker, for they will actively sabotage the mission because the mission is no longer about them.

UNLEARN TOXIC BEHAVIORS

To reiterate a previous point, social learning theory submits that people learn by observing. When hubris leaders are elevated, usually because of their self-promotion campaign, the other organizational citizens take note and replicate not what's displayed on bulletin boards but what they see modeled daily in the workforce. The longer such practices are allowed to linger, the more entrenched it becomes in the culture of the team. Unfortunately, it will take either an intervention or a significant organizational event for citizens as well as stakeholders to accept the fact that they are headed in the wrong direction.

GALVANIZE SERVANT-LEADERSHIP TRAINING

A survey of the literature suggests that when budgets are low, and time is short, the first line item that decreases is training. This trend implies that training is irrelevant and provides little value to the bottom line. Being mindful of this assertion, it is recommended to proactively and systematically galvanize the art and science of leading as servant into the training pipeline of a firm. With the usage of the principles outlined in Chapter Five, one could potentially embrace case studies, guided discussions, videos, and the latest technology to provide the "taught" side of the servant way as others reinforce the "caught" aspects by example.

HABITUALLY COMMUNICATE SERVANT MESSAGES

Communication is perhaps one of the most elusive yet important components of leading. Even when one does not intentionally convey messages, intangibles like silence and body language become the new mechanism of speaking. It would serve a leader well to systematically and creatively launch a servant-leadership communication campaign. Whether one purposefully uses the written platform, such as Lejeune's pointed usage of the words "served" in his book or in a message to the fleet about the relationship between officer and enlisted, leaders should not embrace the communicate-once-and-forget approach. On the contrary, it would be more prudent to employ the rule of seven. The rule of seven in the world of marketing suggests that it will take at least seven marketing messages to reach a prospective customer before one will act on a message. If this is true, then the onus is on the leader to communicate a repetitive message of service and selflessness to this generation of warfighters.

TOAST SERVANT BEHAVIORS

Ken Blanchard is often given credit for the phrase, "Catch people doing something right and praise them." This practice can have tremendous power in the hands of a leader endeavoring to reset a toxic or unhealthy atmosphere. What organizations typically do is actively look for wrong and render negative attention to the behavior. Though that has its place in the short term when infractions are egregious (see Chapter Three), it will not produce the desired effects of sustaining the transformation because whatever we appreciate, will appreciate. Therefore, the final element of the "caught" model is to toast servant behaviors. In other words, when a leader witnesses the led practicing the servant way above and beyond the call of duty, invite the organization to an assembly and give special commendations. This small act will cost a leader nothing, but it will cost the organization everything when it is neglected.

CONCLUSION

Major General Wendell Neville did become the 14th Commandant of the Marine Corps on 28 February 1929. His track record of competence, character, and embodying the servant way is the writer's argument on why he earned Lejeune's endorsement. Regrettably, much of how Neville modeled the servant way as the Commandant will never fully be known due to the lack of records and the fact that he passed away on 8 July 1930 of complications of a major stroke. What we do know, however, is that Lejeune modeled the servant way before him and the limited evidence within this chapter suggests that Neville caught the spirit of this form of influencing, which strongly suggests that those who served under Lejeune had the propensity to serve others when they were in charge. Perhaps Lejeune was particularly thinking about Major General Wendell Neville, to conclude this argument, when he wrote, "Leadership is the sum total of those qualities of intellect, human understanding, and moral character that enables a person to inspire and control a group of people successfully." We will not know until we make it to the gates of glory and we can ask them as they stand watch. For the hymn of the Corps suggests that we, "will find the streets are guarded by the United States Marines." I believe that Major General Wendell Neville would simply answer such a question by saying, "Follow me, as I serve!"

Kneecap to Kneecap Discussion

1. The premise of this chapter is that the ultimate task of a servant-leader is develop others to serve others if/when their moment comes. Think about the people in your life who intentionally developed you. What did they do? Also, think about the people in your circle of influence. How are you intentionally developing them to be servants in the future? Share this with someone.

2. The argument was made that Neville's form of servant-leadership helped to draw out John Quick's autonomous followership. Do you agree or disagree? Please take a position and defend your stance with examples.

3. Reread Neville's Medal of Honor citation. As you examine the excerpt, circle at least three items that impress you. Have a discussion with someone else on how such traits can be built in today's leaders.

4. What is meant by social learning theory? Provide practical examples on how this theory can help or hinder the building of leaders.

5. Reread the principles affiliated with the CAUGHT acronym. Have a conversation on which element(s) of the acronym can help to develop followers in your organization now.

CHAPTER NINE

NO BETTER FRIEND, NO WORSE ENEMY

"While the Marine Corps Expeditionary Force, when landed in a foreign country, is primarily intended to protect the lives and property of American citizens residing there during periods of disorder; it is also intended to benefit and not to oppress the inhabitants of the country where it is serving."

-John A. Lejeune

The final question that a researcher needs to explore to understand whether or not a person is a servant is, Will the least amongst us benefit? In other words, will the society in which the leader served be better off as the result of their form of service? To study this question, the focus will be primarily placed on Lejeune's assignments. On the surface, it may be difficult for a civilian to reconcile this inquiry in the context of the Marine Corps, considering its mission. According to the National Security Act of 1947, the Marine Corps is directed to:

- The seizure or defense of advanced naval bases and other land operations to support naval campaigns.

- The development of tactics, techniques, and equipment used by amphibious landing forces.

- Such other duties as the President may direct.

Assignments	Engagements / Inspections
1891 – 1893 USS Bennington	
1893 – 1897 Norfolk Barracks	
1897 – 1899 USS Cincinnati	Spanish – American War
1899 – 1900 USS Massachusetts	
1900 – 1900 Recruiting Duty Boston, MA	
1900 – 1903 USMC Barracks Pensacola, FL	
1903 – 1903 Headquarters Washington, DC	
1903 – 1903 USS Panther	
1903 – 1904 USS Dixie	Isthmus of Panama
1905 – 1906 USMC Barracks Washington, DC	
1906 – 1906 USS Columbia	Panama
1907 – 1909 Barracks Washington, DC	Philippines
1912 – 1913 USS Ohio	Guantanamo Bay, Panama Canal
1913 – 1913 USS Prairie	
1913 – 1914 2nd Advanced Base Regiment	Veracruz, Mexico
1914 – 1918 Assistant Commandant	
1918 – 1919 2nd Division	WWI
1920 – 1929 Commandant	Haiti, Cuba, Puerto Rico, West Coast
1929 – Death	VMI

TABLE 4 JOHN A. LEJEUNE ASSIGNMENTS

Such guidance can essentially be translated to mean the employment of lethal force to protect and defend the Constitution of the United States from all enemies foreign and domestic. How then can the utilization of lethal means leave a society better off? When such means is employed by a government through the lens of just war, it can indeed be no better friend, no worse enemy. In the specific case of Lejeune, Table 4 depicts the various assignments of the 13th Commandant as well as some milestone engagements. An examination of this table will show that there were three categories of Lejeune's assignments: The Banana Wars, WWI, and preparation in the time of peace.

JUS AD BELLUM

It is only fitting to first briefly outline an objective and historical measure to explore the righteousness of a war. For centuries, the dominant lens policymakers employed to determine whether to utilize lethal force to bend the opposition's will to a political aim has been the just war theory. The just war theory essentially prescribes a framework for nations to go to war, fight in the war, and properly conclude the engagement morally. The aspect that pertains to this conversation will be the justification to go to war, *Jus Ad Bellum*. *Jus Ad Bellum* has four key conditions that must be met for the engagement to be just. The following questions summarize the cruxes of each.

- Just War Question 1 – Have legitimate heads of state formally declared war?

- Just War Question 2 – Is there a just cause to go to war?

- Just War Question 3 – What are the intentions, and are such intentions to go to war just?

- Just War Question 4 – Is going to war the absolute last resort?

Though the above questions are an oversimplification of a very complex theory, they will be used to help determine if societies were left better off while Lejeune served.

BANANA WARS

The first phase of John A. Lejeune's service to the country was primarily in support of the Banana Wars. Such engagements, according to Gilderhurst (2000, p. 49), were "occupations, police actions and interventions on the part of the United States in Central America and the Caribbean between the end of the Spanish War in 1898 and the inception of the Good Neighbor Policy in 1934." With regards to the application of the just war questions, O'Connell (2013) would essentially argue that the Banana Wars were not moral largely due to the intent of the policymakers. Namely, President Wilson's Secretary of State, Robert Lansing indicated on behalf of the country

> I confess that this method of negotiations, with our Marines policing the Haitian capital, is high handed. It does not meet my sense of a nation's sovereign rights and is more or less an exercise of force and an invasion of Haitian independence. From a practical standpoint, however, I cannot but feel that it is the only thing to do as we intend to cure the anarchy and disorder which prevails in that Republic.

Moreover, the president's policy with other Central American nations was to "teach Latin Americans to elect good men." This culture, established from the top down, possibly set the environment for escalated toxicity amongst the people and possibly worsened order when "good men" were not elected as defined by American leadership. This reality is possibly what provoked Lejeune's friend Major General Smedley Butler to assert that war is a racket. This Medal of Honor recipient indicated

> I spent 33 years and 4 months in active military service.... And during that period I spent most of my time as a

high-class muscle man for Big Business, for Wall Street and the bankers. In short, I was a racketeer, a gangster for capitalism. Thus, I helped make Mexico and especially Tampico safe for American oil interests in 1914. I helped make Haiti and Cuba a decent place for the National City Bank boys to collect revenues in. I helped in the raping of half a dozen Central American republics for the benefit of Wall Street. I helped purify Nicaragua for the international banking house of Brown Brothers in 1902–1912. I brought light to the Dominican Republic for American sugar interests in 1916. I helped make Honduras right for American fruit companies in 1903….Our boys were sent off to die with beautiful ideals painted in front of them. No one told them that dollars and cents were the real reason they were marching off to kill and die. (Butler, 1933)

Considering the above, and from the perspective of the Central American and the Caribbean citizens, one would have to conclude that betterment was not the order of the day, due to a lack of moral authority. This assessment illuminates the necessity for executives to embrace the sentiments of President Lincoln—right makes might. When such guidance is clearly embraced, it sets the conditions for truth to permeate, as America's sons and daughters avail themselves to be instruments of moral justice.

WORLD WAR I

The second occupation that involved Lejeune was World War I. Contextually speaking, President Woodrow Wilson employed a policy of neutrality on the war and much of the American population favored this approach as Europe engaged. This disposition slowly changed, however, as several ships were attacked that resulted in the loss of American lives. Though the American ally, Germany, provided a disingenuous apology, that did not subside the outrage. As such

In 1917, Germany, determined to win its war of attrition against the Allies, announced the resumption of unrestricted warfare in war-zone waters. Three days later, the United States broke diplomatic relations with Germany, and just hours after that the American liner Housatonic was sunk by a German U-boat. On February 22, Congress passed a $250 million arms appropriations bill intended to make the United States ready for war. In late March, Germany sunk four more U.S. merchant ships, and on April 2 President Wilson appeared before Congress and called for a declaration of war against Germany. Four days later, his request was granted. (History. com Editors, 2010)

Lejeune's autobiography, *The Reminiscences of a Marine*, spent more time unearthing this aspect of his career than any other. Perhaps this was due largely because of the righteousness that undergirded this warfighting endeavor. In other words, legitimate authority heads of state formally made a declaration of war, the cause was just, the intentions were clear, and it was a last resort. Due to this policy, and with respect to the thousands of lives that gave the ultimate sacrifice, one would have to conclude that the end state improved societal norms.

COMMANDANCY & VMI

The final phase of Lejeune's honorable service to the country included being the 13th Commandant and the Superintendent of VMI. From this platform, this larger-than-life personality prepared the nation for war by instituting a framework that planners in the Corps continue to benefit from to this day. As the top Marine, his vision accessed America's finest and returned them back home as better citizens. Because he loved democracy, he ordered the Marines to protect trains when they were being robbed during his tenure and insisted that these men carry themselves in an honorable manner while at home. His administrative refinement helped Congress to understand the value of military preparation and service as the Superintendent shaped thousands of leaders as they operated in their respective fields. Thus, if one were to invoke the principles of just war in a peacetime environment, then the conclusion would have to be that our society improved.

CONCLUSION

This chapter briefly explored the question, Will the least amongst us benefit, or will the society in which the leader served be better off as the result of their form of service? Three phases of Lejeune's illustrious vocation were examined through the lens of just war theory. Though the Banana Wars didn't adhere to standards and did not warrant an affirmative response, the Corps itself did abstract lessons learned as epitomized in the book *Small Wars Manual*. One of the key lessons that planners learned is that successful campaigns are built on a unified belief in the cause of the campaign (Holmes, 2001). Perhaps it was this message that fueled the spirit of WWI and thereby contributed to the ultimate edification of European society. Finally, Lejeune's work as the commandant as well as the superintendent made America better. Though the lens of just war did not apply, one can glean from history that this Marine made a positive impact. Thus, the sum of the cursory evidence seems to suggest that Lejeune's service to the nation, for the most part, improved societies. This section concludes by reiterating his own thoughts on the matter.

While the Marine Corps Expeditionary Force, when landed in a foreign country, is primarily intended to protect the lives and property of American citizens residing there during periods of disorder; it is also intended to benefit and not to oppress the inhabitants of the country where it is serving. This altruistic conception of the duties of Marines was constantly impressed on the officers and men stationed abroad, with the result that the good will of the law abiding people with whom they were associated was gained and peace and good order were restored and maintained. (Lejeune, 1930, Loc 6301)

Kneecap to Kneecap Discussion

1. It has been said that the ultimate gauge of leadership should not be based on the status of the leader but determined by the condition of the led. If this is true, think about the condition of those you are privileged to lead. Are they becoming better due to your form of influence? What are some practical things you can improve upon starting today?

2. Reread the simplified conditions for a just war. Do you agree or disagree that engagements should be moral as defined by *Jus Ad Bellum*. Please defend your answers with examples. Reflect on the three phases of Lejeune's career (i.e., Banana Wars, WWI, & Commandant/VMI) as well

as President Lincoln's belief that right makes might. How would you communicate such principles in the midst of 21ˢᵗ-century conflicts?

3. Again, Lejeune believed that, "While the Marine Corps Expeditionary Force, when landed in a foreign country, is primarily intended to protect the lives and property of American citizens residing there during periods of disorder; it is also intended to benefit and not to oppress the inhabitants of the country where it is serving. This altruistic conception of the duties of Marines was constantly impressed on the officers and men stationed abroad, with the result that the good will of the law-abiding people with whom they were associated was gained and peace and good order were restored and maintained." Take a position for or against this statement, and defend your point of view with examples.

 CHAPTER TEN

THE SERVANT-LEADER'S BLIND SPOT

"Each day new problems came to me for solution, and unaccustomed difficulties were encountered. To take intelligent action and to make sound decisions necessitated painstaking investigation and much thought."

-John A. Lejeune

As outlined by the above quote from Lejeune, one of the chief responsibilities of a leader is to define reality or to make sound decisions. This notion of defining reality is essentially the art of determining which hill to take and outlining clear courses of action through the prism of principled lenses. Boyd (1976) drills down on this construct and famously frames this process as the OODA loop. As a reminder, Boyd argues that the prelude to decisive action includes observing, or the ability to collect data via various inputs. The orienting aspect speaks to how one makes sense of the data and deciding points toward the art of selecting the right course of action.

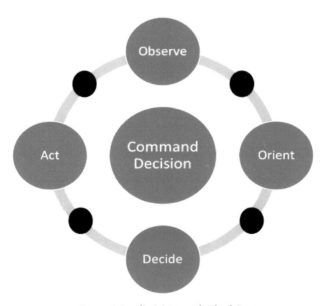

Figure 9 Boyd's OODA with Blind Spots

Though numerous military strategists have embraced Boyd's (1976) model as an authoritative approach to make command decisions, this pathway is not without limitations. As depicted in Figure

9, the OODA loop can become stifled if a leader inadvertently processes information from the platform of blind spots. Leadership blind spots can be defined as a regular tendency to repress, distort, dismiss, or fail to notice information, views, or ideas in a particular area that results in an individual failing to learn, change, or grow in response to changes in that area (Blakely, 2007).

Luft and Ingram (1955) devised a model known as *Johari's Window* to illuminate the blind spot. There are four categories within this concept. The first quadrant is referred to as the "open" element of a leader. This place represents what is known to self as well as what is known to others. An example of this quadrant may be a leader and his followers perceiving a commander to be an approachable influencer.

The second arena is called the "hidden" element. This represents areas where a leader clearly knows about self but deliberately conceals from others. A possible example of this element may be some form of an addiction that typically shocks everyone once it surfaces. The third facet of *Johari's Window* is called the "unknown." The unknown are things not known to others as well as to the leader. Examples of the unknown may include unresolved grief, post-traumatic stress disorder, or other suppressed painful events. It should be noted at this point that private unprocessed pain can become a public leadership problem if it is not confronted in time.

The final element of *Johari's Window* is the blind spot. This leadership weakness is clearly observed by others, but the leader does not acknowledge its existence. Blakeley (2007) describes it best by asserting that, "Leadership blind spots are unproductive behaviors that are invisible to us but glaring to everyone else. Our behavioral blind spots create dire and unintended consequences: They corrupt decision-making, reduce our scope of awareness, create enemies, destroy careers, and sabotage business results. In good times blind spots are annoying and frustrating; in tough times they can be lethal."

The literature suggests there are five possible leadership blind spots that could undermine sound decisions. The first leadership blind spot is having a singular perspective (Maxwell, 2006). An influencer with a singular perspective quickly imposes their will upon others without fully understanding the whole. Usually such leaders are naturally gifted, but such endowment keeps them talking more than listening.

The second leadership blind spot is insecurity. Due to this personality flaw, an influencer seeks to overcompensate in other areas.

The third leadership blind spot is devaluing others. For example, a leader looks down on others simply because they don't hail from a similar educational, economical, ideological, or sociological background. This blind spot, consequently, makes the led feel like an "object," not a person. This tendency tends to destroy overall morale.

The fourth leadership blind spot is an out of control ego. This blind spot forces people in the organization to constantly walk on eggshells, largely out of fear of being the next person to be thrown under the proverbial bus.

The final possible blind spot is burnout. Maslach and Leiter (1997) contend that burnout is the index of the dislocation between what people are and what they have to do. It represents an erosion in values, dignity, spirit, and will—an erosion of the human soul. It is a malady that spreads gradually and continuously over time, pulling people into a downward spiral from which it's hard to recover. Furthermore, Maslach and Leiter suggest that the following factors can contribute to burnout:

- The requirement to do more with less over a sustained period;

- The burden of being micromanaged;

- Insufficient rewards or when someone else takes credit for your efforts;

- A breakdown in a community of support;

LOOKING FOR JOHN A. LEJEUNE

In light of the above cursory review of the literature, the question becomes, What was John A. Lejeune's blind spot(s)? This query is not new. Admirers, scholars, and practitioners alike have pondered the same. Barrow's (1999) article, "Looking for John A. Lejeune," however, is perhaps one of the most focused attempts to present a feasible answer. Barrow, in his own sentiments, went "looking for warts" as he referenced Lejeune's (1930, Loc 6557) statement that "I leave unwritten many things that I ought have written." Fueled with this open door, Barrow sets out to conduct interviews with those who knew the legend best—family, friends, and those who served with him. After numerous hours, Barrow found that Lejeune had a temper. According to the 17th Commandant, General Thomas Holcomb, "[H]e did. But I never heard him swear and I do not recall him raising his voice in anger. When he was angered, he had a rather formidable expression on his face and seemed very much in earnest. There was no doubt in one's mind as to how he felt." Was that a blind spot? This author would argue that having a temper had more to do with being a human, and not with having a bind spot.

Barrow's (1999) research did, however, uncover the first possibility of a blind spot—careerism. The dictionary defines a *careerist* as a person whose main concern is for professional advancement, especially one willing to achieve this by any means. This form of egoism was brought to light when Barrow interviewed the 19th Commandant, General Clifton B. Cates. Barrow captures the essence of the conversation by stating that

> In 1920, Capt Gates, as aide to Gen George Barnett, was in the room when Barnett relinquished the Commandancy to Gen Lejeune but not before the older man stood the younger at attention and chewed him out in the most acrimonious change of command in the history of that high office. To Barnett's charge, as lifelong friends, Lejeune should have warned him of the plot by the Secretary of the Navy Josephus Daniels to remove him from office, Lejeune could only reply, and then repeat, "George, my hands were tied."

Note the phrase, "my hands were tied." This statement implies that he was indeed aware of the plan. If this is true, the questions become, How long was he in the know, and just how involved was Lejeune for the quest for the commandancy? Though we will never know, one could possibly look at his practices and prayers to formulate an evidence-based conclusion.

THE CONVENING OF THE VIGILANCE COMMITTEE

In Chapter Seven a case was made for an important life lesson that Lejeune acquired from his beloved father. Namely, when practices were not being done in a just way, start up a vigilance committee to impose your will. One can see evidence of this practice at the Naval Academy when he became a Marine as well as when he served as a commanding general in WWI. Thus, if this is indeed the propensity of Lejeune, then one shouldn't be too surprised if the 13th Commandant employed his Southern charm and "recruited" the likes of the U.S. Representative Thomas S. Butler, the father of Major General Smedley D. Butler, and Secretary of the Navy Josephus Daniels to serve on his board. Assuming this is factual, were his hands tied because his committee members bound him to secrecy as they did his bidding for him?

THE LEJEUNIAN PRAYER

Another form of circumstantial evidence that Lejeune struggled with the blind spot of careerism, which is a form of egoism, can be found in his prayers. Consider the following supplication that he prayed regularly:

> Every night of my life, I pray to God to take from my heart all thought of self or personal advancement, and to make me able to do my full duty as a man and as a General towards my [Marines] and my country. (Lejeune, 1930, Loc 4049)

From a theological perspective, one does not typically invoke God's help for things that don't present a challenge. For example, one would not have to pray for the Lord's help to not use profane language if one didn't, like Lejeune, swear. The average person petitions God for help with the things in which they struggle. In Gabe's case, his prayer revolved around thoughts of self or personal advancement. As one examines the heart of this leader, it would not be too farfetched to speculate whether his ambition (i.e., thought of self or personal advancement) got the best of him and he actively planned with the influential members of his vigilance committee to usurp the 12th Commandant. After all, was it not Barrow (1999) that pointed out the following ideology of Lejeune? "Some men," argued Lejeune, "are born to ride on other people's shoulders, and others are born to supply the shoulders." Though history proves his shoulders ultimately strengthened the Corps, did it have to be fortified in such a manner?

DEVALUING PEOPLE

The second possible blind spot of Lejeune revolved around the notion of devaluing people. To recap, devaluing occurs when a leader looks down on others simply because they don't hail from a similar educational, economical, ideological, or sociological background. One can see glimpses of Lejeune's deep-seated worldview when he wrote calmly and methodically the following:

> I have briefly described some of the incidents connected with the reconstruction period in order to indicate the difficult conditions under which the people lived and to demonstrate the indisputable fact that it is impossible, except by the use of military force, to maintain a **backward race** in power over a **superior race** [emphasis mine]. To attempt to do so was not only unwise, but was the cause of much ill will, sorrow and suffering. The wounds caused by reconstruction required a much longer time in which to heal than did those resulting from the war between states. (Lejeune, 1930, Loc 266)

What did Lejeune exactly mean by the terms *backward* and *superior* race? Was he thinking of the "ignorant blacks" (Lejeune, 1930, Loc 222), as he called them, that were elected to govern when he was a boy in Louisiana? Was he reflecting about the slaves that worked on their plantation who had enough of being dehumanized and unsuccessfully attempted to stand up their own version of a vigilance committee? Was Lejeune thinking about the "mammie that was obtained who assumed a very dominating position" in their family (Loc 1424–1435)? Was Lejeune reflecting on the numerous letters sent to him from his good friend Smedley Butler that regularly made fun of the African-American plight (Butler, 1989, Loc 1320)? One will never know with complete certainty, but reasonable minds would have to agree that Lejeune had an unhealthy implicit bias. In the era in which he operated, this devaluing posture didn't present a problem due to the geo-political realities of his day. That is, this way of thinking was the norm and permeated from the highest level of government as epitomized with the showing of the best-selling 1915 movie *The Birth of a Nation* that debuted from the White House. (*The Birth of a Nation* is a movie that depicts blacks as backwards and whites as a superior race. Moreover, this movie celebrates the KKK as an American tool of justice.) It should be noted, however, that had Lejeune led with this blind spot in today's context, he would have been amongst the 70% relieved of duty due to bias (Seck, 2018).

BURNOUT

The third possible blind spot of Lejeune emerged toward the twilight of his career. Bartlett (1991) best captures it when he wrote

> As Lejeune approached the end of his second term as commandant (5 March 1929), he felt serious misgivings about the condition of his Marine Corps. Although almost everyone expected Lejeune to serve another term, the weight of the office began to tire him. Lejeune's personal appearance suggested that he had begun to lose that special pride in his uniform; he appeared rumpled and disheveled at times and began to gain weight. More important, Lejeune grew weary over the unrealistic decisions of Congress. (Loc 166)

The intangible effects of burnout over a course of time will eventually manifest. In Lejeune's case, it can be argued that this erosion of the soul began to display itself toward the end of his career. That is, the 13th Commandant advertised his weariness with his weight, lack of pride in his uniform, and his frustrations with congressional deliberations. The reader should be reminded that Lejeune was a fierce proponent of the belief that the well-dressed soldier exemplified an elevated level of morale. To this end, for this leader to no longer take pride suggests that Gabe was running on empty and that his edge was becoming dull.

A 5-POINT PLAN TO RECALIBRATE JUDGMENT
In light of the above discussion about Lejeune's possible blind spot, the question now becomes, What measures should an emerging influencer employ to assure their judgment is fit to lead? The first answer to such an inquiry can be abstracted from a business practice utilized at The Basic School (TBS). More specifically, this entity that is charged with the training and education of newly commissioned Marine officers ensures that such leaders will be "able to decide… in the fog of war." A soft tool that is employed to achieve this objective is their version of a 360-degree feedback assessment. Hollenbeck (1997) defines the 360-degree feedback method as the "process of feeding back to a person (usually a manager or executive) how others see him or her. The others are typically bosses, peers, and direct reports; sometimes they are others outside the immediate organization, for instance, internal or external customers" (p. ix).

During their 26 weeks of warfighting training, the Marines are required to provide an assessment of their peer's overall leadership. In other words, the DNA of the Marine Corps is to facilitate leadership learning from the platform of raw feedback. If embraced, such advice equips the Marine to become a better officer. To this end, if 360-degree feedback is good enough to shape a young Marine lieutenant, certainly it can help a company commander become more efficient. If 360-degree feedback can refine the officership of a young Marine, then certainly it can recalibrate the judgment of emerging regimental / battalion commanders. If 360-degree feedback is good enough to be within the DNA of TBS, then certainly this tool can help general officers continue to grow.

It has been said that the more senior a person becomes, the less likely followers will tell the truth to their face. If this is true, we are missing out on some priceless sage advice that can only propel our leadership ability to the next level. To this end, the first recommendation to newly selected officers for command is to take a 360-degree feedback survey. A casual internet search will reveal a litany of credible firms that conduct this service at a minimal price. It is better to receive up-to-date, objective knowledge about one's limitations and strengths than to allow such traits to undermine the organization. For the sake of the Marines and sailors that you have the privilege of leading, allow this author to challenge you today to mitigate those blind spots and reinforce strengths with this invaluable tool.

EXECUTIVE COACH

I will never forget that embarrassing moment when I played defensive back (DB) in college. It was a big game, and our beloved DB coach had us in a bump and run the entire day (a form of defensive strategy that calls for close man-to-man coverage). It was 2nd down and a long 15 yards to go on their 30-yard line, and like any good DB / WR squabble, there was a lot of trash talking. I recall the WR saying something to the effect of making me look bad (this is the PG13 version) and me assuring him that would not happen. After the ball was snapped, I recall delivering an aggressive bump and being right in his hip pocket when the ball was thrown. The next thing I recall was the referee signaling touchdown! When I approached the sideline in frustration, the DB coach basically said I let him off the line without even touching him. I immediately refuted the claim and argued that not only did I jam him, it was a great blow. After minutes of arguing, my coach said, "Wait until Monday, and I'll show you exactly what you did!" To which I replied, "Can't wait!"

When Monday rolled around, the DB coach called me into his office and showed the play in slow motion. The film revealed that the WR essentially slapped my helmet and then pushed off. This technique gave him the advantage he needed to score. In the moment, unfortunately, I confused the impact of the slap with what I perceived as a jam. In other words, until that moment I was operating with several "athletic" blind spots. It took the skill set of my DB coach to help me accept reality, learn from my mistake, and employ new skills. In like manner, it is recommended that commanders proactively seek out a confidential executive coach before assuming command.

The objective of this second recommendation is to facilitate learning with a leader based upon goals that enhance professional and personal satisfaction as well as overall effectiveness over a contracted period. Corbett and Colemon (2005) suggest that quality executive coaching utilizes the following steps:

Taking Stock – During this phase, the focus is placed on taking stock of a leader's strengths, weaknesses, gifts, and motivations. This is usually done by way of a 360-degree survey and other personality tools.

Environment Examination – During this phase, the environment in which the leader serves is assessed. As noted by one newly selected commander, "We have the command climate surveys in place. But really this captures the environment the previous CO created. What would be a good gesture is to have this survey done maybe a year into your tenure. That will better help to gauge the climate under your leadership as opposed to the previous guy's." Regardless, an executive coach can help to understand the perceptions of coworkers, bosses, and followers, and compare those with the awareness of the client.

Behavior Goal Setting – During this phase, the client is given the proper space and time to set goals based upon feedback. This step is critical because it serves as a cornerstone for the rest of the unfolding process.

Personal Development Plan – At this point, the executive coach works with the client to establish realistic goals to help them move from one point to another.

Accountability – Over a set period of time, the client gives the coach permission to hold them accountable to agreed-upon goals.

Celebration – The final element of the coaching process involves celebrating achieving objectives.

Even though I got beat on the field that day, that season with my DB coach literally transformed my career. In a similar vein, I am convinced that time invested with a quality executive coach can proactively prevent and lessen battlefield blunders, address leadership blind spots, and help commanders become more deserving of that special trust and confidence that is vested upon the office. For the sake of the country, allow me to challenge you to reach out today to a seasoned coach that can take your game to the next level.

KEEP ME GROUNDED

The name of the painting is simply called the *Loneliness of Command*. This famous piece, painted by Mort Kunstler, depicts General Robert E. Lee as he observes from his tent. What is fascinating about the painting is the fact that no other person is around, and his tent is uninviting. In other words, it appears that General Lee had an open door policy that everyone knew was really closed. The nuances affiliated with his environment coupled with perhaps his own style of influencing set the conditions for the following phrase to apply—"It's lonely at the top." When leaders invoke this saying, they are usually trying to describe their inability to open up to people in the chain of command, peers, and supervisors about their true concerns.

Maxwell (1998) argues, however, that if a leader does feel lonely at the top, then they are doing something wrong. The solution to this problem, Maxwell contends, is "getting off the top and going where the people are." In the context of command, some of the people to go to may include the executive officer, chief of staff, the senior enlisted advisor, or even the chaplain. Giving these key command stakeholders the "permission" to keep you grounded while you are in command can very well be the difference between command success and failure. To this end, this third recommendation of allowing others to proactively hold you accountable in love can reinforce leadership lessons abstracted from your season with an executive coach.

LIFELONG LEARNER

The fourth recommendation to refine one's judgment springs from the notion of being a lifelong learner. Bluntly put, we are either green and growing, or ripe and spoiling. One sure way to exercise the ethical muscle is to engage our minds. To this end, a good learning objective is to commit to reading a book or an article, or to listen to some form of growth-focused lecture monthly. As such, the following recommended readings may serve emerging leaders well as they assume more responsibility.

- *How the Mighty Fall* by Jim Collins
- *Blink* by Malcolm Gladwell
- *Think Again* by Sydney Finkelstein, Jo Whitehead, and Andrew Campbell
- *You're in Charge, Now What?* by Thomas J. Neff and James M. Citrin
- *Leadership Blind Spots* by Karen Blackely
- *The Maxwell Daily Reader* by John C. Maxwell
- *A Tactical Ethic* by Dick Couch
- *Leading the Charge* by General Tony Zinni
- *The Courageous Follower* by Ira Chaleff
- *Overcoming the Five Dysfunctions of a Team* by Patrick Lencioni
- *Transparency* by Warren Bennis, Daniel Goleman, and James O'Toole
- *Servant Leadership* by Robert K. Greenleaf
- *Bold Followership: A Biblical Cure for Organizational Toxicity* by Maurice A. Buford

SPIRITUALITY

The advice from John A. Lejeune serves as the final recommendation to refine judgment. Lejeune, upon observing the realities of combat, famously wrote that, "There is no substitute for the spiritual in warfare." It was as if this leader of Marines understood that one's training and personal skill sets can only take one so far, particularly in the fog of war. Therefore, leaders should be open to search beyond what one can do on their own or within oneself and to reach out to a greater power.

IS YOUR OODA LOOP CALIBRATED?

The followers under your charge deserve an honest answer to the following question, Is your OODA Loop calibrated? To recap, an unsynchronized OODA loop can blur one's judgment and undermine overall command efficiency. Fortunately, tools like 360-degree surveys, executive coaching, command accountability, lifelong learning, and spirituality can help to ensure that one's judgment is on point. Because the wars of the now, as well as the future, will be played out in a very visible way, it would behoove leaders of Marines and others in general to consider embracing the recommendations of this section. The return on investment can be as high as "keeping our honor clean."

To close out this argument, the possible blind spots of Lejeune were not brought to light during his career. Whether or not this was a positive or not goes beyond the scope of this publication. The key takeaway of this chapter is that no leader is beyond having a blind spot, even a servant-leader. Servants do, however, have the propensity to be more open to seeking self-improvement with humility for personal as well as organizational efficiency.

Kneecap to Kneecap Discussion

1. Considering the five major blind spots of leaders, which one tends to be the dominant one in your organization? Please defend your answer with examples.

2. A case was made for three possible blind spots for Lejeune. Please discuss if you believe (or not) such issues would undermine his judgment in today's context. Provide examples.

3. Take a position for or against the statement—"It's lonely at the top." Discuss what leaders should do to address this tendency.

4. A model was provided for a leader to address blind spots. Select an element on that model that would be most challenging and explain why.

THE ETERNAL SPIRIT IN THE 21ST CENTURY

"With it we also received from them the eternal spirit which has animated our Corps from generation to generation and has long been the distinguishing mark of Marines in every age."

-John A. Lejeune

Marine Corps University hosted a panel discussion in 2018 with five senior Marines on the topic, "The Spiritual Imperatives of Command." One of the panelists, SgtMaj Gary Smith, made a provocative statement when he was asked about his thoughts on the subject. This motivator stated that, "Whatever is down in that well, will come up in the bucket." This metaphor pointed toward a rural mannerism that suggests that if a person lowers the lever on the well and icy water is present, that is what will come up. In like manner, if the well is full of dirty water or no water at all, that is what will come up in the bucket. As such, the remaining questions of this book are, What was in the well of John A. Lejeune, how did this substance help him to shape the trajectory of the Corps, and what can this generation of warfighters learn from this effort? To explore these inquiries, consider the following sentiments.

> My son, I do not expect to see you again. I have had this thought throughout the months you have been at home and do not seem to be able to throw it off....I have mentioned this because I want to talk seriously with you before you go out into a strange environment where the restraining influences of the Naval Academy and your mother and father will be lacking. For many years I had no church affiliations and gave but little thought to religion. During recent years, however, I have been slowly but steadily forced to the conviction that a religion which has produced a woman of such beautiful character as your mother must be a good religion. Now, my son, hold fast to the religion which your mother has taught you, and do not forget her love, her precepts, or her example. (Lejeune, 1930, Loc 598)

While on leave from Annapolis, his 68-year-old father provided the above benediction over the life of his son before he passed away a brief time later. From the perspective of this father, he was convinced that there was positive relationship between faith and character. But what exactly did Lejeune's mother teach her son, and what possible precepts did the 13th Commandant abstract from a woman with such a beautiful character?

THE FAITH OF A MOTHER

Young John A. Lejeune learned a plethora of lessons from his mother. The former Ms. Laura Archer Turpin was a deeply religious and most loving mother who was reared under the strictest Presbyterian influence. At the age of seven, Lejeune's mother essentially homeschooled him due to the lack of academic institutes in the community. According to Gabe,

> Religious as well as secular instruction formed an important part of the school curriculum. My mother was entirely free from all forms of religious intolerance or bigotry. She taught the Protestant children their catechisms, and with the approval of the Catholic priest of the nearby church she prepared the Catholic children for their confirmation and first communion and on his visitations was complimented by the Archbishop on the thorough manner in which she had instructed them. She was greatly beloved by all the children and by their parents as well, and her memory is so deeply reverenced by those who knew her as to make me feel that her spirit still lingers in the community as an influence for good. (Lejeune, 1930, Loc 211)

One can argue that his mother nurtured in him a deep abiding faith, an appreciation for the role of a teacher and scholar, as well as a set of values that forever shaped his worldview.

THE FAITH OF A COMMANDANT

The counsel from his father and the example of his mother took root as young Lejeune navigated his way through life. Bartlett (1991) illuminates this point by indicating that, "Family dinners, especially on Sunday, became traditional times of fellowship. Each gathering began with prayers as Lejeune became increasingly religious. A devout Episcopalian, he and his family became members of a local church no matter where his duties took him" (Loc 50). His faith, unquestionably, persuaded him to not become a drunkard (Loc 1232) and to live a life of integrity. Lejeune's faith, it should be noted, was not restricted to the confines of the four walls of the church. On the contrary, he integrated his faith into the virtues of being a Marine in several ways.

First, Lejeune invoked prayers to help him mitigate his blind spots. To recall a previous point, Gabe wrote that "every night of my life, I pray to God to take from my heart all thought of self or personal advancement, and to make me able to do my full duty as a man and as a General towards my [Marines] and my country" (Lejeune, 1930, Loc 4049). Second, Lejeune offered praise to the Lord at the cease of battle. He explains that, "We were satisfied with the terms of the Armistice. We were happy because fighting, death and destruction had ceased. I offered up a prayer of thanksgiving to Almighty God" (Loc 5461). Third, Lejeune actively encouraged the officers in the Corps "to devote their close attention to the many questions affecting the comfort, health, morals, religious guidance." Fourth, Lejeune would often use religious rhetoric to inspire the troops. The following address given to the troops during WWI on Thanksgiving Day at the request of Chaplain Pierce best summarizes this point.

This is the day set apart by our forefathers as Thanksgiving Day. Each year the President issues a Thanksgiving proclamation, setting forth the reasons we have had during the preceding twelve months for being thankful, and calling on all our people to assemble in their places of worship and give thanks to God for the blessings which they have received. The President's proclamation is always read at these services. This year, owing to our rapid advance towards Germany, the proclamation has not yet reached us, and we are deprived of the privilege of hearing it read. Our Chaplain, therefore, has asked me to act as a substitute and to say a few words to you about this Thanksgiving Day. I feel that it is needless for me to tell you why our Division, our Army, and our people at home should be thankful today. All of you know the story of how our country has, as if by magic, been organized for war; of how our army has been trained, supplied and transported overseas without loss; and when, at the end of the month of May, Germany was at the height of its power and its path to conquest seemed clear, all of you know the story of how this splendid Division of fighting men, with their hearts inspired with patriotism, filled with burning zeal, and steeled with divine courage, was deployed on his front, checked his advance, and then defeated the enemy. All of you know the story of how, since those days, he has met defeat after defeat, and how, only a few days ago, he was finally forced humbly to beg for peace. Truly it was the handiwork of God. It is, therefore, very fitting that we should gather together today and give thanks to the Lord God of Hosts for having given our nation and our cause this speedy and this decisive victory, and for having selected us to be among the instruments chosen by Him to carry out His will. (Lejeune, 1930, Loc 5741–5752)

Finally, Lejeune understood the necessity of faith when one is engaged in a lethal campaign. Specially he states that,

In war, if a man is to keep his sanity, he must come to regard death as being just as normal as life and hold himself always in readiness, mentally and spiritually, to answer the call of the grim reaper whenever fate decrees that his hour has struck. It is only by means of this state of mind and soul that a man can devote all his thoughts, all his intellect, and his will to the execution of the task confided to him....While war is terribly destructive, monstrously cruel, and horrible beyond expression, it nevertheless causes the divine spark in men to glow, to kindle, and to burst into a living flame, and enables them to attain heights of devotion to duty, sheer heroism, and sublime unselfishness that in all probability they would never have reached in the prosecution of peaceful pursuits. Sherman's alleged definition is correct, by thousands, aye millions, of the men who have engaged in war have shown themselves to be truly the children of God. (Lejeune, 1930, Loc 4321–4332)

A possible inference from this quote is that mental toughness and spirituality are critical components to the mind-set of a warrior. When such constructs are intentionally interwoven into the training and education of a soldier of the sea, they become steeled with divine courage and a heavenly spark flings upward. Such a catalyst can be a contagious asset on the battlefield or in the boardroom as it generates sheer heroism and inspiring magnanimity. Thus, the well of Lejeune's soul was filled with the principles of Judeo-Christian scripture.

REKINDLING THE ETERNAL SPIRIT

A cursory review of today's headlines would suggest that the moral fiber of the nation weighs in the balance. Because warriors hail from this context, the military is not immune from recent trends in the larger society. This reality has caused military influencers to scrabble for solutions, but such answers are either faddish at best or totally inept at worst. This reality begs the question on how warfighting organizations can best be morally revitalized. The beginning quote of this chapter offers a possible solution. Lejeune tells us, "[W]e also received from them the eternal spirit which has animated our Corps from generation to generation and has long been the distinguishing mark of Marines in every age." This rhetoric of eternal spirit should not be surprising coming from this man with a strong Judeo-Christian worldview. From a theological perspective, the term *spirit* can be synonymous with fire. As illustrated in Figure 11, there are three key elements of fire: oxygen, heat, and fuel. When a spark is ignited in the context of all necessary variables, a robust fire ensues. In a similar vein, to invigorate organizational morality, certain leadership constructs must be enacted.

Figure 11 The Key Elements of Fire

THE OXYGEN OF TRUST

The first essential component is trust. As Chapter Two outlined, this intangible facet of leadership cannot be overlooked. Conventional wisdom suggests that top leaders often use their positions or the power of the pen to get followership to trust the organizational vision. This technique (i.e., leading by fear only) is often short lived because the team needs to trust the vision caster before they will embrace the vision. In other words, to rekindle Lejeune's notion of an eternal spirit, influencers must understand the top question of followership. Namely, the research suggests that followers are asking, Can I trust you? They want to know that you will not abuse your authority. They are curious if they can follow your judgment, especially in the fog of war. Followers are constantly watching to gauge whether your public rhetoric matches your private behavior. Thus, to cultivate an environment of trust, it must be earned daily.

HANDLING THE HEAT

The second element of fire is heat. Metaphorically speaking, this points toward a construct known as leader member exchange (LMX). LMX illuminates the space between the leader and the led. How well an influencer manages this space will determine the efficiency of that command. As mentioned in Chapter Six, the best way to impact this area is to eat last. Eating last without an agenda is an additional way to earn trust and to model what right looks like. Though it takes more strength of character, more discipline, and focus to break selfish tendencies, it will make the difference when defining moments emerge.

THE FUEL OF INSPIRATION: HERO MAKERS

The final component of fire is fuel. Fuel is the sustaining variable that enables the fire to continuously burn. In like manner, inspiration is critical to leadership. The Latin root of the word inspiration is *inspirare*. *In-* means "to infuse," and *spirare* is "the breath of life (spirit)." Plainly put, inspiration is the act of exciting, influencing, or arousing another into action. There are two ways that influencers can inspire followers in the 21st century. The first principle can be abstracted from Robert Kelley's book *The Power of Followership*. Kelley's research revealed that followers want their leaders to be less of a hero and more of a hero maker. Leaders can become less of a hero and more of a hero maker by

- Investing resources into the led that will help them win at work and life;

- Giving the led the autonomy to grow;

- Helping the led to better understand their "why";

- Holding the led accountable in private;

- Publicly giving credit and praise to the led.

Second, leaders can be an inspiration by cultivating their own sense of *spirare*. Like Lejeune, a leader's well needs to be healthy and full enough to sustain them as they embrace the weight of command and lead souls into combat. At the end of the day, one can't give, what one doesn't have. Thus, to be an inspiration, a leader must first become spiritually fit.

CONCLUSION

This book examines the original writings of Lieutenant General John Archer Lejeune as well as other source documents to answer the questions, What leadership traits did Lejeune model during war as well as peacetime, and can this example help the 21st-century warrior engage the opposition, inspire the information-age Marine, and motivate followers on the battlefield as well as the boardroom? While applying Robert Greenleaf's "best test," the evidence outlined in this book suggests that Lejeune led as a servant. Additionally, the literature shows that though he employed the principles of a servant-leader, he was not without flaws. Specifically, Lejeune had some glaring blind spots that were not challenged.

Regarding the questions, Can this example help the 21st-century warrior engage the opposition, inspire the information-age Marine, and motivate followers on the battlefield as well as the boardroom, the answer is—it depends. It is largely contingent on each leader's courage to look within to understand their implicit biases and to work through such barriers for the good of the organization. Without this fortitude, the eternal spirit will slowly fade, and the greatness of the team will not be actualized. But when a leader eats last, embraces spirituality, and surrounds themselves with a team unafraid to detect blind spots, that command will transition from good to great. The remaining question now becomes, Do you have the courage to embrace the servant way?

Kneecap to Kneecap Discussion

1. "Whatever is down in that well, will come up in the bucket" (SgtMaj Gary Smith). Reflect on this statement and give examples of this occurring in the life of a leader as well as yourself.

2. Recall the last words of Lejeune's father. Discuss the role upbringing (good, bad, or indifferent) has on leadership formation.

3. Take a position for or against the question, Can the eternal spirit be rekindled in the 21st century? Be sure to defend your position with evidence.

4. Hero makers do many things: invest resources, give the led autonomy to grow, hold the led accountable in private, and publicly give credit and praise to followers. Discuss why this stance of the hero maker is important in today's organization.

Adam, Hajo, and Adam D. Galinsky. 2012. "Enclothed cognition." *Journal of Experimental Social Psychology,* July 918-925.

Anonymous. 1931. "Signaling in the Corps." *Marine Corps Gazette* 15(5).

Asprey, Robert B. 1962. "John A. Lejeune: True Soldier." *The Marine Corps Gazette.* —. 1962. "John A. Lejeune: True Soldier." *Marine Corps Gazette.* April. Accessed August 16, 2018. https://www.mca-marines.org/gazette/ john-lejeune-true-soldier.

Baldor, Lolita C. 2013. *Sex is Major Reason Military Commanders are Fired.* 01 21. Accessed July 26, 2018. https://www. military.com/daily-news/2013/01/21/sex-is-major-reason-military-commanders-are-fired.html.

Ballendorf, Dirk Anthony, and Merill Lewis Bartlett. 1997. "Pete Ellis: An Amphibious Warfare Prophet, 1880-1923." *Annapolis: Naval Institute Press* 28-47.

Bandura, Albert. 1977. *Social Learning Theory.* New York: General Learning Press.

Barrow, Clayton. 1990. "Looking for John A. Lejeune." *Marine Corps Gazette.* April. Accessed September 22, 2018. https:// www.mca-marines.org/gazette/looing-john-lejeune.

Bartlett, Merrill L. 1991. *A Marine's Life: Lejeune 1867-1942.* Annapolis, Maryland: Naval Institute Press.

Baruto, J., and R. Hayden. 2011. "Testing Relationships Between Servant Leadership Dimensions and Leader Member

Exchange (LMX)." *Journal of Leadership Education,* 10(2): 22-37.

Bates, Ralf S. 2014. "Leadership, John Lejeune Style." *Marine Corps Gazette,* 98(11). November. Accessed December 18, 2017. https://www.mca-marines.org/gazette/2014/11/leadership-john-lejeune-style.

Bates, Ralph Stoney. 2013. *A Marine Called GABE: The Life and Legend of John Archer Lejeune, The Greatest Leatherneck of Them All.* North Charleston: CreateSpace Independent Publishing Platform.

Blakely, Karen. 2007. *Leadership Blind Spots.* San Francisco: Jossey-Bass.

Blanchard, K. 2000. "Leadership by the Book." *Executive Excellence,* 17(3): 4-5.

Boyd, John. 1976. *Destruction and Creation.* US Army Command and General Staff College.

Brown, J. L., D. Sheffield, M. R. Leary, and M. E. Robinson. 2003. "Social Support and Experimental Pain." *Psychosomatic Medicine* 65(2): 276-283.

Buford, Maurice A. 2018. *Bold Followership: A Bibical Cure for Organizational Toxicity.* Cham, Switzerland: Palgrave Macmillan.—. 2018. *Bold Followership: A Biblical Cure For Organizational Toxicity.* Cham, Switzerland: Palgrave Macmillan. —. 2012. *The Controlled discipline of servant leaders: A qualitative study.* Regent University: ProQuest (UMI Dissertations Publishing, 3515406).

Buford, Maurice A., Doris Gomez, Kathleen Patterson, and Bruce E. Winston. 2014. "The Controlled Discipline of Servant Leaders: A Qualitative Study." In *Servant leadership:*

Research and Practice, by Raj Selladurai and Shawn
Carraher, 24-46. Hershey, PA: IGI Global.

Butler, Smedley D. 1987. *Maverick Marine*. Lexington: The
University Press of Kentucky.

Butler, Smedley. 1933. "Intervention Speech."

Castro, Carl Andrew, Charles W. Hoge, Charles W. Milliken,
Dennis McGurk, Amy B. Adler, Anthony Cox, and Paul D.
Bliese. 2006. *Battlemind Training: Transitioning Home from
Combat*. MD: Walter Reed Army Institute of Research.
Accessed May 21, 2018. file:///C:/Users/Maurice%20
Buford/Downloads/Battlemind_training_Transitioning_
home_from_combat.pdf.

Chapman, Gary, and Paul White. 2011. *The 5 Languages of
Appreciation in the Workplace: Empowering Organizations
by Encouraging People*. Chicago: Northfield Publishing.

Cialdini, Robert B. 2009. *Influence*. New York: Harper
Collins Publishers.

Collins, J. 2001. *Good to Great*. New York: Harper Business.

Conger, J. A. 1992. *Learning to Lead: The Art of Transforming
Managers into Leaders*. San Francisco: Jossey-Bass.

Corbett, B., and J. Colemon. 2005. *The Sherpa Guide: Process-
Driven Executive Coaching*. Ohio: Thomson.

Covey, Stephen M. R. 2006. *The Speed of Trust*. New York:
Free Press.

Covey, Stephen. 2006. *The Speed of Trust*. New York: Free Press.

Dierendonck, Dirk Van, and Kathleen Patterson. 2010. *Servant
Leadership: Developments in Theory and Research*. New
York, NY: Palgrave and Macmillan.

Dunn, Elizabeth W., Lara B. Aknin, and Michael I. Norton. 2002. "Prosocial Spending and Happiness: Using Money to Benefit Others Pays Off." *Harvard University.* Accessed May 9. http://nrs.harvard.edu/urn-3:HUL.InstRepos:11189976.

Eisenberg, Eric M., H. L. Goodall, and Angela Tretheway. 2007. *Organizational Communication: Balancing Creativity and Constraint.* Boston: Bedford/St. Martin's.

Frank, Benis M. 1972. "The Relief of General Barnett." *Records of the Columbia Historical Society, Washington, D.C.* 679-693.

Gilderhurst, Mark T. 2000. *The Second Century: U.S. Latin American Relations Since 1889.* Wilmington: Scholarly Resources Inc.

Gladwell, Malcolm. 2008. *Outliers: The Story of Success.* New York: Little, Brown and Company.

Greenleaf, Robert K. 1977. *Servant Leadership: A Journey into the Nature of Legitimate Power and Greatness.* New York: Paulist Press.

Greenleaf, Robert. 1977. *Servant Leadership.* Mahwah, NJ: Paulist Press.

Heath, Elena. 2014. "Active vs. Passive Learning." November 6. Accessed March 14, 2016. https//prezi.com/m/oguxiz0h5hh8/active-vs-passive-learning/.

History.com. 2010. "America enters World War I." *HISTORY.* February 9. Accessed September 21, 2018. https://www.history.com/this-day-in-history/america-enters-world-war-i.

Holmes, Richard. 2001. *The Oxford Companion to Military History.* Oxford: Oxford University Press.

Howard, Michael, and Peter Paret. 1984. *On War: Carl Von Clausewitz.* Princeton: Princeton University Press.

Huang, Haifeng. 2017. "A War of (Mis)Information: The Political Effects of Rumors and Rumor Rebuttals in an Authoritarian Country." *British Journal of Political Science; Cambridge* 47(2): 283-311.

Iarocci, Joe. 2018. July 2. Accessed August 23, 2018. https://serve-leadnow.com/greenleafs-best-test-servant-leader/.

Irving, J. A., and G. L. Longbothem. 2007. "Servant Leadership Predictors of Team Effectiveness: Findings and Implications." *Journal of Business and Behavioral Sciences,* 15: 82-94.

Kaplan, S. 2000. "Human Nature and Environmentally Responsible Behavior." *Journal of Social Issues,* 56: 491-505.

Kelinske, Bonnie, Brad W. Mayer, and Kuo-Lane Chen. 2001. "Perceived benefits from participation in sports: a gender study." *Women in Management Review,* 16(2): 75-84.

Kelley, Robert E. 1998. "Leadership Secrets From Exemplary Followers." In *Leading Organizations: Perspectives For A New Era,* by Gill R. Hickman, 193-201. Thousand Oaks: SAGE Publications, Inc.

Kelley, Robert. 1988. "In Praise of Followers." *Harvard Business Review.* November. Accessed September 6, 2018. https://hbr.org/1988/11/in-praise-of-followers.

Kotter, John P. 2012. *Leading Change.* Boston: Harvard Business Review Press.

Krulak, Charles C. 1999. "The Strategic Corporal: Leadership in the Three Block War." *Marines Magazine,* January.

Krulak, Victor H. 1984. *First To Fight.* Annapolis: BLUEJACKET BOOKS.

Kuhn, Thomas. 1996. *The structure of scientific revolutions (3rd ed).* Chicago: The University of Chicago Press.

Lee, Gus, and Diane Elliott-Lee. 2006. *Courage: The Backbone of Leadership.* San Francisco: Jossey-Bass.

Lejeune, John A. 2016. "A legacy of esprit and leadership." *Marine Corps Gazette,* March 80-85.

Lejeune, John A. 1922. *Kindly and Just: Letter No. 1.* Washington, DC: United States Marine Corps. —. 1920. *Relations Between Officers and Men.* Washington, D.C.: United States Marine Corps. —. 1920. "Special Trust and Confidence." *Marine Corps University.* Accessed April 2, 2018. https://www.usmcu.edu/historydivision/special-trust-and-confidence. —. 1930. *The Reminiscences of A Marine [Kindle Version].* Philadelphia: Dorrance and Company.

Lencioni, Patrick. 2006. *Silos, Politics, and Turf Wars.* San Franciso: Jossey-Bass.

Lichten.valner, Ben. 2013. "Fortune's Best Companies to Work For With Servant Leadership." *Modern Servant Leader.* May 4. Accessed May 7, 2016. http://modernservantleader.com/servant-leadership/fortunes-best-companies-to-work-for-with-servant-leadership/.

Luft, Joseph, and Harrington Ingham. 1955. *The Johari Window, a graphic model of interpersonal awareness.* Los Angeles: UCLA.

Maslach, Christian, and Michael P. Leiter. 1997. *The Truth About Burnout.* San Francisco: Jossey-Bass Inc.

Maxwell, John C. 1998. *The 21 Irrefutable Laws of Leadership*. New York: Thomas Nelson.

Maxwell, John C. 2006. "The Blind Spot Lecture Series." Atlanta: IMPACT.

McShane, Steven L., and MaryAnn V. Glinow. 2013. *Organizational Behavior: Emerging Knowledge. Global Reality*. New York: McGraw-Hill Irwin.

Meyer, Dakota, and Bing West. 2012. *Into the Fire: A Firsthand Account of the Most Extraordinary Battle in the Afghan War*. New York: Random House.

Mittleman, Murray. 1998. "Study: Stress of firing someone doubles the risk of a heart attack." *Associated Press*. March 20. Accessed June 8, 2018. http://chronicle.augusta.com/ stories/1989/03/20/bus_224461.shtml. —. n.d. "The Associated Press."

Moss, Rob. 2013. "Personnel Today." *The 11 most common issues raised at a disciplinary hearing*. September 24. Accessed June 4, 2018. https://www.personneltoday.com/hr/the-11-most-common-issues-raised-at-a-disciplinary-hearing/.

Norton, Richard. 2008. *John Archer Lejeune: The Cajun Who Saved The Corps (A Case Study)*. Rhode Island: Naval War College.

O'Connell, Aaron. 2013. *U.S. Marines In The Banana Wars*. Annapolis, March 26.

Patterson, Kathleen. 2010. "Servant Leadership and Love." In *Servant Leadership: Developments in Theory and Research*, by Dirk Van Dierendonck and Kathleen Patterson, 67-76. New York, NY: Palgrave and Macmillan. —. 2003. *Servant leadership: A theoretical model.* Doctoral dissertation: Dissertation Abstracts International, 64/02, 570.

Phillips, Stone. 2004. "Dateline NBC." *Can humility, fatih be good for business?* February 28. Accessed May 14, 2016. http://www.nbcnews.com/id/4374722/ns/dateline_nbc/t/can-hu-mility-faith-be-good-business/#.Vzeq0Y-cGUk.

Rems, Alan. 2017. "Semper Fidelis: Defending the Marine Corps." *U.S. Naval Institute.* June. Accessed June 12, 2018. https//www.usni.org/magazines/navalhistory/2017-06/semper-fidelis-defending-marine-corps.

Research, Pew. 2014. "Millennials increasingly are driving the growth of 'nones.'" May. Accessed March 5, 2016. http://www.pewresearch.org/fact-tank/2015/05/12/millennials-increasingly-are-driving-growth-of-nones/.

Rowe, James N., Daniel Lee Pitzer, and Humbert R. Versace. 1969. "Five Years as a Viet Cong Prisoner." *Army Digest* 24(5): 4.

Russell, Joyce. 2016. "Staying calm under pressure tells a lot about a leader." *LA Times.* June 19. Accessed September 6, 2018. http://www.latimes.com/business/la-fi-on-leadership-calm-20160618-snap-story.html.

Ryan, Kathleen D., and Daniel K. Oestreich. 1998. *Driving FEAR Out of the Workplace: Creating the High-Trust, High-Performance Organization.* San Francisco: Jossey-Bass.

Sandage, S., and T. W. Wiens. 2001, Fall. "Contextualizing models of humility and forgiveness: A reply to Gassin." *Journal of Psychology and Theology* 29(3): 201-219.

Savage-Austin, A., and A. Honeycutt. 2011. "Servant Leadership: A Phenomenological Study of Practices, Experiences,

Organizational Effectiveness and Barriers." *Journal of Business & Economics Research*, 9(1): 49-54.

Seck, Hope Hodge. 2018. *70 Percent of Marine Commander Firings This Year Due to Bias, Disrespect.* September 13. Accessed September 27, 2018. https://www.military.com/daily-news/2018/09/13/70-percent-marine-commander-firings-year-due-bias-disrespect.html.

Tanja de Jong, Noortje Wiezer, Marjolein de Weerd, Karina Nielsen, Pauliina Mattila-Holappa and Zosia Mockałło. 2016. "The impact of restructuring on employee well-being: a systematic review of longitudinal studies." *Work and Stress* 30(1): 91-114.

Tuckman, B. W., and M. Jensen. 1977. "Stages of Small Group Development Revisited." *Groups and Organization Studies* 419-427.

USMC. 1999. "Marine Corps University." *Corporals Noncommissioned Officers Program.* January. Accessed May 2, 2018. http://www.militarytraining.net/Cpl%20Course/Classes/Drill%20102.PDF.

USMC_History_Division. 2002. "Sergent Major John H. Quick." *USMC History Division.* January 22. Accessed August 26, 2018. https://web.archive.org/web/20110615062750/http://www.tecom.usmc.mil/HD/Whos_Who/Quick_JH.htm.

Venzon, Ann Cipriano, and Martin Gordon. 2008. *Leaders Of Men: Ten Marines Who Changed the Corps.* Lanham: The Scarecrow Press, Inc.

Vrabel, Jeff. 2012. *Why Are There So Many Bad Bosses? Some People Are Natural-Born Leaders. Others Are Cruel, Inhuman Monsters.* Towers Watson Global Workforce Study, Success.

Wick, Robert J. 2005. *Spiritual Resilience.* Cincinnati: Franciscan Media.

Winston, Bruce. 2002. *Be a Leader for God's Sake.* Virginia Beach, VA: Regent University-School of Leadership Studies.

Winston, Bruce E. 2008. "Leading biblically: Controlled discipline." Accessed June 5, 2018. http://ww.boundless.org/2005/articles/a0001688.cfm.

Wis, R. 2002. "The conductor as servant leader." *Music Educators Journal* 89(17).

Yukl, Gary A. 2002. *Leadership in Organizations.* New Jersey: Prentice-Hall.

Yukl, Gary. 2010. *Leading in Organizations.* New Jersey: Prentice Hall.

Zak, Paul J. 2017. *Trust Factor: The Science of Creating High-Performance Companies.* New York: AMACOM.